W9-BKU-966

The Burn Cookbook

BURN
#MEANGRILLS

AN UNAUTHORIZED UNOFFICIAL COOKBOOK FOR MEAN GIRLS FANS

the Burn Cookbook

A Parody

REAL RECIPES TO FEED YOUR INNER PLASTIC

Jonathan Bennett
& Nikki Martin

Foreword by Lacey Chabert

GRAND CENTRAL
Life & Style

Cover design by Ashley Prine, Tandem Books

Additional copyright information can be found on page 167.

Hachette Book Group
1290 Avenue of the Americas, New York, NY 10104
grandcentrallifeandstyle.com
twitter.com/grandcentralpub

First Edition: October 2018

Grand Central Life & Style is an imprint of Grand Central Publishing. The Grand Central Life & Style name and logo are trademarks of Hachette Book Group, Inc.

Print book interior design by Ashley Prine, Tandem Books
Illustrations by A. Collins, Tandem Books
Photograph on page xii is courtesy of Jonathan Bennett
Photographs on pages 57, 121, 125, 130, 133, and 175 are by Kharen Hill.
All other photographs are by Brent Weber.

Library of Congress Cataloging-in-Publication Data

Names: Bennett, Jonathan, 1981- author. | Martin, Nikki, 1980- author.
Title: The Burn Cookbook : An Unofficial Unauthorized Cookbook for *Mean Girls* Fans / Jonathan Bennett and Nikki Martin.
Other titles: Burn book | Burn cookbook
Description: New York : Grand Central Publishing Life & Style, [2018] |
Includes index.
Identifiers: LCCN 2018016625| ISBN 978-1-5387-4730-8 (hardcover) | ISBN 978-1-5387-4732-2 (ebook)
Subjects: LCSH: Cooking. | Mean girls (Motion picture) | LCGFT: Literary cookbooks.
Classification: LCC TX714 .B3894 2018 | DDC 641.5—dc23
LC record available at https://lccn.loc.gov/2018016625

ISBNs: 978-1-5387-4730-8 (hardcover); 978-1-5387-4732-2 (ebook)

Printed in the United States of America

LSC-C

10 9 8 7 6 5 4 3 2 1

This book is dedicated to anyone who has ever been personally victimized by a Regina George.

And to Marci Liroff, Tina Fey, Lorne Michaels, and Mark Waters. You have changed my life like you wouldn't believe. Thank you for taking a kid from Ohio and making his dreams come true.

And lastly to my mom and dad. I miss you both and wish you were here for this adventure.

—JONATHAN

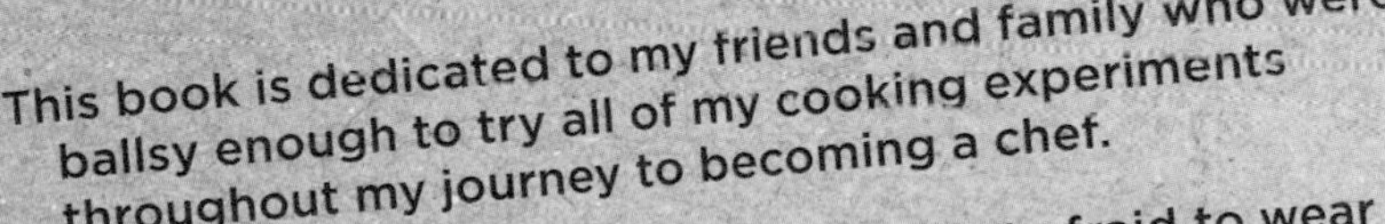

This book is dedicated to my friends and family who were ballsy enough to try all of my cooking experiments throughout my journey to becoming a chef.

And to all the guys and gals out there not afraid to wear an apron, get messy, maybe even set your hair on fire, and actually make something instead of ordering Postmates. #BossBabes #WifeMaterial

—Nikki

Contents

Foreword by Lacey Chabert viii

Introduction ix

Own Your Kitchen 2

- CHAPTER 1 -

Whore d'Oeuvres | 9

So, You Agree? Fairy Toast 10

Gretchen's Wieners 12

Whatever, I'm Getting Cheese Fries 14

White Gold Hoops 16

Spring Fling Rolls 18

Cheese and Crackers for Eight People 20

I Can't Help That I'm So POPular Popcorn 22

It's Not Regular Guac, It's Cool Guac 24

- CHAPTER 2 -

Regina's All-Carb Diet | 31

Swedish Nutrition Bars 32

Are Buttermilk Pancakes a Carb? 34

Your (Angel) Hair Looks Sexy Pushed Back 36

Fetch-uccini Alfredo 38

Mac and Cheese Balls, Because I'm a Mouse, Duh 40

Is Your Cornbread Muffin Buttered? 42

- CHAPTER 3 -

I Really Want to Lose Three Pounds | 47

Just Stab Caesar Salad 48

Boo You Whore-iental Salad 50

Grool Sleepover Oats 52

Three-Days-'til-Spring Fling Cranberry Fat Flush 54

You Smell Like a Baby Prosti-turmeric Latte 55

You Will Get Pregnant and Diet Smoothie 56

- CHAPTER 4 -

On Wednesdays We Eat, Drink, and Wear Pink | 61

I Want My Pink Soup Back! Watermelon Gazpacho 62

She's Fabulous, but She's Evil. And These Are Her Deviled Eggs. 64

Burn Brunch Citrus Salad 66

I'm Sorry People Are So Jealous of My Perfect Pink Taco 68

Give Me a Beet Hummus 70

Queen Beet-za 72

Strawberry Frosé, Obvi 74

Not Word Salad. Actual Pink Salad. 76

Do Not Trust These Treats 78

- CHAPTER 5 -

Cramming for Finals | 83

Aaron Samuels's Actual Mom's Chicken Stuffed Shells 84

JAMBO-laya 87

Total Meltdown 90

She Asked Me How to Spell *Orange* Chicken 92

October 3-Bean White Chili 94

Why Are You So Obsessed with MEatloaf? 96

It's Like, All in Swedish Meatballs 98

- CHAPTER 6 -

Mean Grills (She Doesn't Even Grill Here) | 105

Amber D'Alessio Grilled Hot Dogs 106

Best. Rack. Ever. 107

Everyone Grab Some RubBURGERs 109

Hot as Africa Pepper Chicken 112

Homeschooled Jungle Veggie Bowl 114

- CHAPTER 7 -

Happy Hour Is from Four to Six | 119

Why Are You White? Russian 120

Regulation Hottie Toddy 122

Test Results on the Rocks 123

Too Gay to Function Cosmo 124

Awesome Shooters 126

High Status Man-hattan Candy 128

You Can't Sip with Us 130

You Go, Glenn (Hot) Coco 131

Half a Virgin Piña Colada 132

- CHAPTER 8 -

Get In, Loser, It's Desserts | 137

Cake Made of Rainbows and Smiles 138

The Fun-Fetchy Cake 141

Face Smells Like a Foot Peppermint Bark 144

Hump Day Treat: Peanut Butter BALLS 146

Ms. Norberry Pie 148

Strawberry Toaster Doodles 152

Crack Rock Candy 154

Milkshake-It Like 2004 156

Final Thoughts 164

Acknowledgments 166

Index 168

FETCH

Foreword

In 2003, I was fortunate to be cast as Gretchen Wieners in *Mean Girls*. I use the word *fortunate* not only because the movie would go on to be loved for years to come, but while filming it, I made some wonderful friends. One of those very special people is Jonathan Bennett. When he asked me to write this foreword, I became very nostalgic about meeting him on set in Toronto all those years ago. I remember being instantly taken by his infectious laugh and his zest for life. One of my favorite qualities about Jonathan is that he manages to turn every experience into an adventure! While filming we became very close. I'm proud to say, all these years later, we remain great friends.

We've not only acted alongside one another in various projects since, but we've celebrated many of life's milestones together throughout the years. Whether it's a birthday or holiday, Jonathan always makes sure to celebrate the occasion to the fullest! So many of these celebrations, which have now become fond memories, have been centered around a delicious meal, and maybe a cocktail or two ;). It only seems fitting that Jonathan, of all people, would write a cookbook as fun as this one!

I believe fans of the Plastics will love this cookbook. The recipes are fun and easy to make and will bring you and your group of friends closer together. The charm and excitement that Jonathan brings to life is infused throughout the pages of this cookbook. I hope you enjoy hanging out with him and will gather your group of friends to reminisce and laugh . . . even if you don't go here.

Congratulations to my dear friend Jonathan and cheers to all who will undoubtedly enjoy this cookbook!

Love,

-Lacey Chabert

Introduction

HEY! IT'S ME JONATHAN BENNETT, you met me as that man candy from *Mean Girls*, aka Aaron Samuels. You know, the one who only cares about school, his mom, and his friends. I know that before we go any further, I should probably answer some of your questions and just get them out of the way. So here we go:

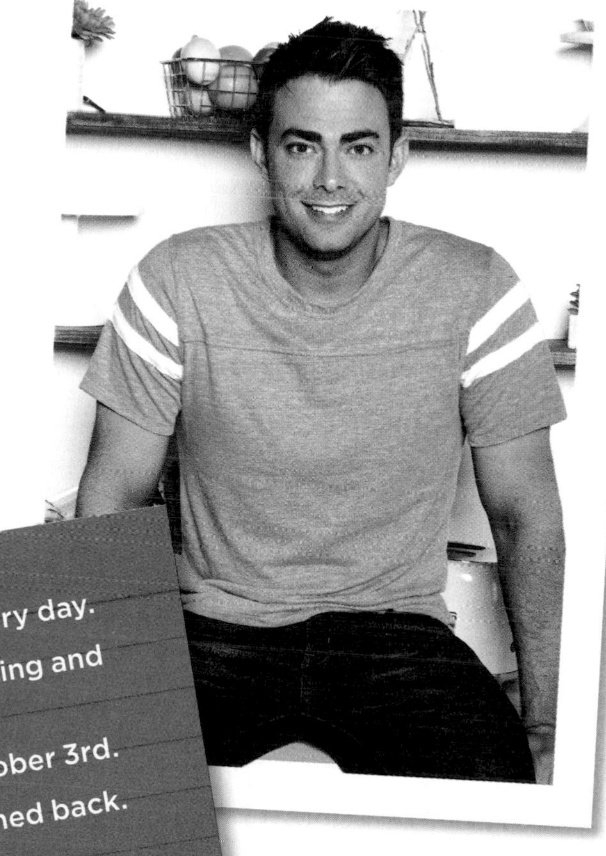

??
?

A. No, I don't hang out with Lindsay every day.
B. Yes, Rachel McAdams is just as amazing and cool as you had hoped.
C. I am aware of what day it is: it's October 3rd.
D. Yes, I know my hair looks sexy pushed back.
E. No, I'm not actually good at math.
F. Hard as she tried, Gretchen Wieners couldn't get "fetch" to happen at North Shore. But since the movie came out, it has become an iconic phrase in pop culture.

As I write this, it has been almost fifteen years since the release of *Mean Girls*, the hilarious, provocative, instantly iconic high school send up. A lot has changed since 2004, but this movie is as relevant as ever: the characters just as memorable, the jokes just as funny, and the satire of girl world as accurate as ever. No matter where you would have sat in the lunchroom, there's something in that movie for everybody.

Now you may be wondering, why after all these years have I decided to write about my time as Aaron Samuels? And why do it through a cookbook, when the girls of North Shore couldn't find their way around the kitchen if the Spring Fling crown depended on it? I wanted to poke a little fun at the world of North Shore and pull some juicy, behind-the-scenes secrets out of Gretchen's hair to share them with you.

The girls in the movie are obsessed with image, and nowhere is that more apparent than in their relationship with food and dieting. In today's world of social media, it feels like everybody's trying to show off their *awesome* meals, with their *awesome* friends on their *awesome* vacations to places more *awesome* than wherever everyone else is. Everybody's playing a role, whether it's pretending that it didn't take twenty tries to get the perfect snap or that dinner didn't go cold while they looked for the best filter. I think one of the reasons *Mean Girls* has the staying power that it does (aside from the incredible script and outstanding acting, natch) is that it serves as a reminder that we're all better when we take ourselves a little less seriously and embrace what makes us each unique. And since I love food, what better way to inspire others than through a delicious set of recipes that also pay tribute to my favorite movie of all time?

One of the reasons that food is so important to me is because of how it connects me to my mother. Throughout my entire acting career, whether I was on stage in a community theater production or on screen for the ABC soap *All My Children*, my mother found a way to share her homemade cooking with the cast and crew. A long tech rehearsal wasn't the same until Ruthanne showed up with enough of her famous Chicken Stuffed Shells, and no cast party (always at our house) was had without her Mandarin Orange Salad (see our version on page 50). Her food brought people together, no matter how late rehearsal was going, or how much drama had taken place behind the scenes. Food was her way of showing me that she was my biggest fan and would support me through everything, and that's why I believe that there's no better way to bring people together than through a delicious, comforting meal.

In 2004, I got to take my mom to the premiere of *Mean Girls* in Hollywood. She stood in awe next to me on the red carpet with her signature smile plastered on her face. Granted, I'm pretty sure deep down this was the proudest of me she had ever been in her life, but her reaction was the same one she'd flash whenever I did anything she could boast to friends and family about.

My mother passed away in 2012, and when I was cleaning out her kitchen and I came across the many recipes that she had created over the years. Everything was handwritten on envelopes and scrap paper—many had missing pieces and were impossible to decipher. I wanted to make sure as many of her recipes as possible lived on forever and weren't lost over time.

That's where my Food Network pal, Nikki Martin, who must have had ESPN or something, stepped in! She was able to resurrect my mom's recipes and use her magic touch to turn them into masterpieces.

Jam-packed with recipes, this book speaks to more than just your stomach. The recipes are delicious and the drinks are fetch and serve way beyond four to six.

We also have exciting new games and quizzes that will turn your regular, basic brunches into so much fun that even Principal Duvall will think you've gone wild. *You girls have gone wild!*

The Burn Cookbook has been created so you can bring your friends together to share and relive the moments of everyone's favorite movie, *Mean Girls*. This is a way to embark on a new adventure and see if you have what it takes to sit with us.

So rather than obsess over your man shoulders, huge calves, or bad breath, I want you to celebrate with these delicious recipes that will make you laugh about your favorite scenes in a new way. Because real talk: food really does have the potential to help us all get along like we did in middle school. So, grab your friends, put your hair up (but remember you can only wear a ponytail once a week), and start cooking! Don't worry, even if it's a complete disaster, you can always just get cheese fries.

LOVE YA, BEYOTCHES!

Now go shave your back.

The Burn Cookbook

Own Your Kitchen

JAMBO, WOULD-BE CHEFS! Welcome to your kitchen! Ya know, that room in the house where you keep your wine, beer, box of Tums, and last night's pizza? Well, guess what? It's about to become your new BFF. We are going to be doing wild and crazy things up in here . . . like BAKING, SAUTÉING, SIMMERING, ROASTING, MIXING, BLANCHING, BOILING, and even GRILLING!

WARNING: It will get hot and you will get dirty, but it will all be worth it. You'll impress new friends, maybe even score a BF or GF, and—most importantly—save some cash by eating and getting drunk at home, all with the new skills you're about to learn.

I like to think of the kitchen and its contents as similar to a good old-fashioned Caboodle. (Remember Caboodles? Those super-cute, everyone-had-to-have plastic makeup cases? The ones where you kept all your important beauty sh*t along with other top secret stuff? Google it.) Well, just like with the Caboodle, if the kitchen isn't well stocked with the right tools and essentials the end result isn't gonna be pretty. And all of us mean girls just want it to be pretty, right? So here's a basic list for the basic chef's Kitchen Caboodle:

APRON: Your food is only as good as you look. If I'm looking and feeling super-awesome, my PMA (positive mental attitude) is through the roof and just permeates everything I make and do. So don't be a fugly, grumpy chef. Be a hot and sassy one, full of confidence, rainbows, and smiles. (If you can't do this naturally, start drinking wine before you preheat your oven and that should help with your PMA.) I always have a few aprons at the ready so I can look and feel like I know what I'm doing and avoid getting marinara sauce all over my new skinny jeans.

SALT: It's fundamental. It's even elemental. (But you probably skipped Chem 101, didn't you?) There are many types you can use while cooking, I like to have my kitchen

NEW YORK
SELTZER

stocked with traditional sea salt or fleur de sel, and pink Himalayan salt. The sea salt has a lovely and gentle taste that is great for finishing grilled meats and most dishes. The pink stuff, well for one it's F-ing *pink,* so there's that. And nutritionally, it's better than the regular stuff so why not go for it? Did I mention that it's pink?

KNIVES: Get a good one. Go now. We'll wait. FACT: You are far less likely to cut your damn acrylics off with a sharp knife than a dull one. I know sharp = scary, but a dull knife can slip and drag and do way more damage to your digits and food as you use it. You don't need that many either. A small serrated knife is essential for things like bread and tomatoes and a heavy duty 7-inch chef's knife is perfect for heavy duty work like chopping. Add a laser sharp paring knife and you're good to go.

NONSTICK PAN: This pan will save your life. Get one that is "green" or nontoxic. You can find these for sale at your local Bed Bath & Beyond. (Use a coupon!) I love my GreenPan cookware and in fact I have a couple of pans in different sizes. Your fried eggs will magically slip off, pancakes will never stick, and even fish will crisp but not leave scales.

CAST IRON PAN: This is must-have kitchen item. Get one that is pre-seasoned—I personally love the Lodge brand and use it for everything. A super-hot cast iron pan will give your meat the sexiest, most even char, and leave the perfect golden crust on a fillet of fish. You have to care for your cast iron like you would a pair of Gucci pumps, but the results are always worth it. Cast iron pans are especially good for when you want that grilled flavor and char but it's too cold outside to actually stand at a grill. Or, better yet, you can use your cast iron *on* the grill to do veggies while your shrimp is cooking. So versatile. It even subs as a weapon against intruders or pervy creepy Tinder dates—one smack on the head and *lights out*, a-hole!

MEASURING CUPS AND SPOONS: I mean, how else will you measure stuff? Get a set and put them in a handy drawer because you will be using them often. Look for a tempered glass measuring cup for liquids and a set of regular cups and spoons for measuring dry ingredients.

RIMMED BAKING SHEETS: Grab a few different kinds, you won't regret it. Invest in two full-size, two half-size, and a couple more quarter-size ones. You can multitask with these babies: from baking cookies, roasting veggies, and blistering tomatoes to melting cheese on bread. Just don't get flat baking sheets. Don't even bother. The rims on rimmed baking sheets prevent spillage and make you look like a pro. Less spillage = less mess on cute outfit. Got it?

OTHER MUST-HAVE TOOLS: A can opener, a veggie peeler, a wine bottle opener, a couple of durable spatulas, wooden spoons, a candy thermometer and a meat thermometer, a whisk, a microplane, a mandoline, and two sets of metal tongs (a long one for grilling, preferably with rubber handles, and a shorter one for pan frying).

APPLIANCES: There are so many gadgets and electronics out there, I promise you don't need them all. Half of what you see in the store is just random counter clutter. Find basic multitaskers that actually get the job done. (Also, stay away from 99 percent of the "As Seen on TV" kitchen things, too.) What you actually need:

- Toaster: Because toast.

- Supercharged blender: A good one can puree, and make soup, smoothies, and cool mom blended margaritas!

- Hand mixer: Think whipped cream, mashed taters . . . the list goes on and on.

- Mini food processor: Works like a charm for quick and easy minced or diced garlic, onion, or shallots. Especially helpful for those of you with obnoxiously long nails or scary knife skills.

- Rice cooker: Burnt rice is gross. Even as a professional, I still burn rice. I love my rice cooker. I use it for all kinds of grains, such as quinoa, farro, and couscous. Just drop the ingredients in, turn it on and set it, and walk away. Leaves so much more time for selfies and Instagram stories.

In addition to the gear, you're going to need some pantry basics to take your cooking game to the next level.

Pantry Essentials

EXTRA VIRGIN OLIVE OIL: *Puh-lease* get a good one. It's worth the extra few dollars since this is going into basically everything. Avoid the crappy and cheap basic grocery brands. Most of the cheapy stuff is blended—not even really olive oil—and can be highly rancid if it's been on the shelf too long. Look for something that is cold pressed, organic, and has a peppery finish. The more an olive oil tickles your throat when you taste it, the higher the plyphenol content is, which is a good thing. It all equals antioxidants and free radical healthy stuff. Trust.

NEUTRAL OIL: Don't waste that high-class olive oil! If you're making dressings or frying stuff, go neutral. Some recipes here call for canola; it's not my favorite oil, but it is practically flavorless and it's easy to find. I also like having coconut and avocado oils on deck because they are loaded with good-for-you fats.

NONSTICK COOKING SPRAY: Ladies, this is like the primer to your foundation! So many recipes will call for this: Add it to your next shopping trip. If you're new to cooking it's especially important to err on the side of caution and use that spray like a can of Aqua Net. Don't ruin a dish by having half of it stuck to the bottom of your pan. Nonstick spray works wonders and there are some great healthier options like coconut oil spray and olive oil spray.

FLOUR: All-purpose flour will cover you for most of the recipes in this book. If gluten isn't your friend, there are a ton of gluten-free all-purpose flours that can be subbed in almost any recipe. Even though I am okay to eat gluten, I often sub gluten-free and it makes my treats like breads and muffins feel less sinful. Your call.

SPICE RACK: Your rack will take you places, I promise. Personally, I like to flavor my food with fresh herbs as often as I can, but there are a few must-have dried spices that every Plastic needs to kick up their dishes. Think: flavor flavor flavor. The most common complaint about food is that it's underseasoned. Don't be shy, spice it up! Here are my favs: cumin, chili powder, garlic powder, bay leaves, oregano, red pepper flakes, herbs de Provence, smoked paprika, dried thyme, turmeric, and cinnamon.

Now that you've outfitted your space and gotten your essentials in order . . . PLEASE remember:

SAFETY FIRST. Go get a fire extinguisher, read the instructions, and have it nearby *just in case*. Also have a first aid kit in your house: the smallest cuts bleed the most. If you do cut yourself, a BandAid covered with a non-latex glove is the easiest way to ensure sanitary food. One time I microplaned my middle finger while I was filming the show *Chopped* and I almost got *chopped.* Nobody wants a finger in their salad.

All right friends, now that we have become better acquainted with our kitchens and, hopefully, have stocked them up with the good stuff, let's get cooking! Remember, practice makes perfect; don't get discouraged. Invite your army of skanks over often to try out new dishes. Make it fun. Just remember, there *will* be fires, blackened steaks, burnt cookies, and spilled milk, but as the old adage goes . . . never cry over spilled milk. However, you *can* cry over fried extensions or getting red wine on your new white Coachella jumpsuit—just not over milk.

Have fun, and remember the people who love to eat are always the best people.

CHEERS!

—Chef Nikki

SMEG

-CHAPTER 1-

Whore d' Oeuvres

Now listen up, Plastics, your days of cutting up cheese sandwiches into fours and handing them out Glenn Coco–style, like they're F-ing candy-grams, are now over. Life is all about first impressions. The same goes for a meal. So, we are introducing you to recipes for the most delicious starters you've ever tasted—ones that may even impress all your new friends. I mean, thank God you finally have some. Just make sure you follow these recipes to a tee. You don't want to scare everyone away like you always do. I mean, you must be getting sick of having to go with your parents to the Ladysmith Black Mambazo concert every weekend. God, that's embarrassing. Consider these recipes your ticket to a real Saturday night.

Remember, whore d'oeuvres are meant to be served at the very beginning of a meal and not in-between courses (or your mom's chest hair!), so make sure you have them ready to go before your guests arrive. No one wants to sit around making small talk with people they hate while the host is running around the kitchen like a chicken with its head cut off trying to get the first course ready.

Now, how many of these awesome appetizers is everyone going to devour? The limit does not exist, so make sure you prepare enough. Whether it's Gretchen's Wieners or It's Not Regular Guac, It's Cool Guac, one thing is for sure: Your nailbeds will still suck and your pores will still be too big. Now hop in loser, let's get cooking.

So, You Agree? Fairy Toast

If Gretchen's father invented Toaster Strudel, then Karen's father definitely would have invented Fairy Toast.

These slices of fabulous have all the qualities of a Karen in toast form. They're colorful, they sparkle, and you don't have to be smart to make them. Use your fifth sense to design them anyway you want, just make sure your letters aren't backwards, or you'll have to put your entire fist in your mouth.

SERVES 4

WHAT YA NEED

4 slices of the whitest bread possible

Butter, like the real deal

Rainbow sprinkles

FETCH FACTS

To whoever made this movie: You dirty little liar! *Mean Girls* is set in Evanston, Illinois, but the movie was mostly shot in Toronto, Canada, at Etobicoke Collegiate Institute and Malvern Collegiate Institute, as well as at Montclair High School in Montclair, New Jersey. Other notable Toronto landmarks featured are the Convocation Hall at the University of Toronto and Sherway Gardens.

☆ MAKE IT ☆

So, you agree? You think you're pretty or you just love to eat things that are pretty?

- Start with the bread: Straightforward white bread will do the trick. Toast the bread to your desired crispness (or don't toast it at all; I don't know your life). Trim the crusts off, no one likes crusts and it's prettier that way. Next, smooth a nice solid layer of butter over your slices, and do not try to get away with that "I Can't Believe . . ." stuff. You know what I'm talking about. Pony up, use real butter.
- Here comes the fun: Cover your buttered slices with hundreds and thousands of rainbow sprinkles. Slice into cute triangles or little squares and place on your prettiest of party platters.

Note: Enjoy with a sparkling rosé, obvi.

Gretchen's Wieners

Why should Amber D'Alessio have all the fun?

Ex-boyfriends may be off limits, but these lip-smacking pigs in a blanket sure aren't! This recipe is, like, so good even Jason won't know what hit him (even though we know—it was that F-ing boom box).

MAKES 24 WEINERS

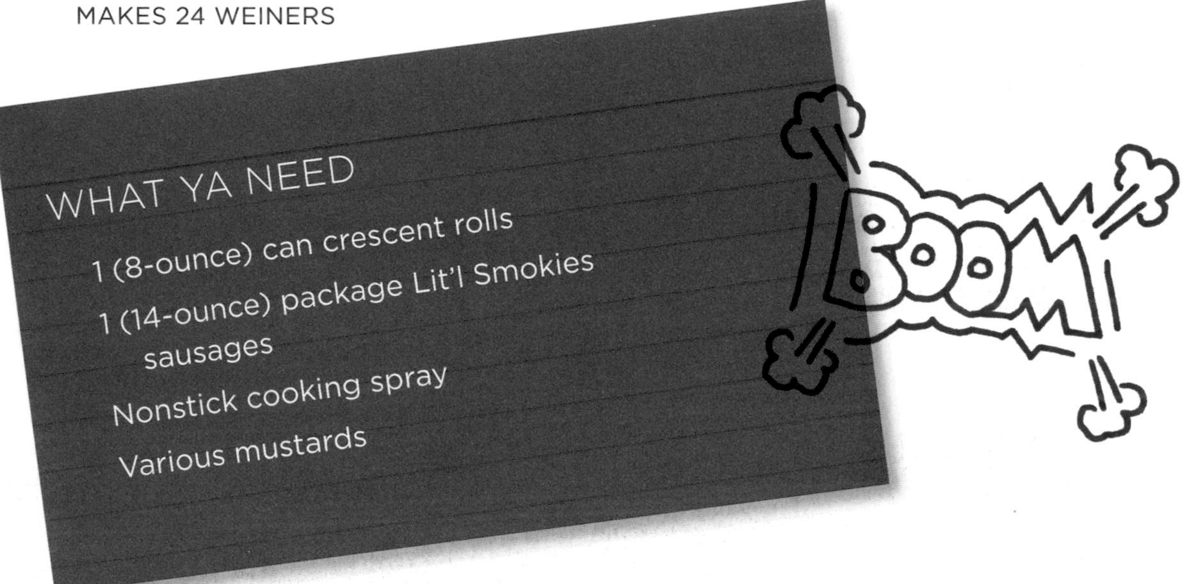

WHAT YA NEED

- 1 (8-ounce) can crescent rolls
- 1 (14-ounce) package Lit'l Smokies sausages
- Nonstick cooking spray
- Various mustards

MAKE IT

Get your oven and aprons on beyotches! Nothing screams P-A-R-T-A-Y more than a pile of hot weiners, *amirite?*

- Preheat oven to 375°F. Open the can of crescent rolls and separate the 8 triangles out on a cutting board, then slice each triangle into 3 narrow triangles, so you should have a total of 24. (Because, math.) Place each Lit'l Smokie on the fat end of a triangle and roll it up. Place on a baking sheet that has been hit with a spritz of nonstick spray. Bake until golden brown, 12 to 15 minutes.

- Serve with a variety of fun mustards for your dipping pleasure and enjoy!

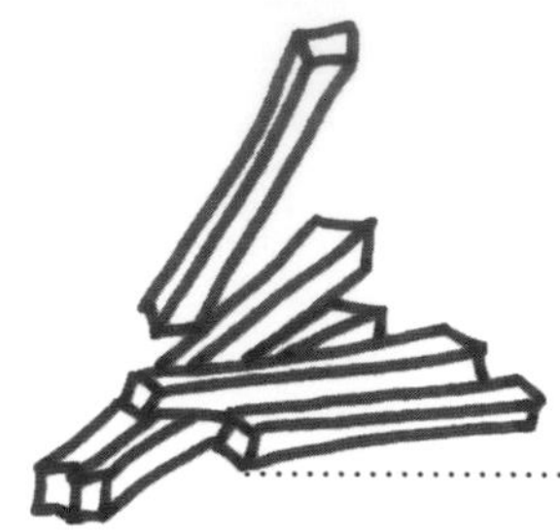

Whatever, I'm Getting Cheese Fries

When all you want to do is eat your feelings.

These nacho-inspired cheese fries are a no-brainer. Why would you even sit there for like one second suffering, when you could be indulging in some hearty emotional eating? Your fat ass will thank you.

MAKES 4 SAD COWS HAPPY ONES

WHAT YA NEED

FOR THE FRIES
- 2 pounds frozen sweet potato fries
- 1 cup frozen sweet corn
- Kosher salt

FOR THE CREMA
- ½ cup plain Greek yogurt
- ¼ cup mashed avocado
- 2 tablespoons minced fresh jalapeños
- 1 tablespoon fresh lime juice
- Pinch sea salt

TOPPING IDEAS
- 1½ cups shredded Monterey Jack cheese
- Canned black beans
- Red onion, diced
- Pickled jalapeño slices

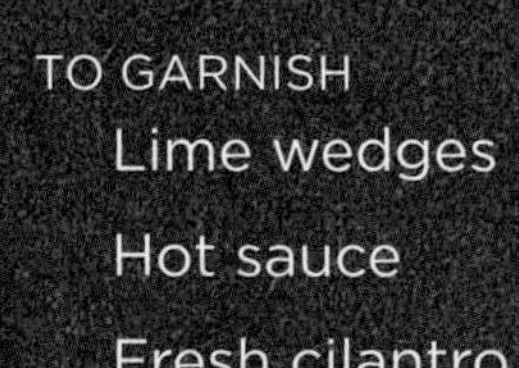

TO GARNISH
- Lime wedges
- Hot sauce
- Fresh cilantro

- Start by getting your oven to a nice 425°F. Bake your fries for about 20 minutes, until crispy, or according to package instructions. Spread corn on separate baking sheet with a pinch of salt and bake along with the fries for about the same time, or until they become charred in a few spots.

- While the corn and fries are cooking, whip up your crema: Combine all crema ingredients in a mini food processor and blend 'til smooth; set aside.

- Once the fries and corn are finished, go ahead and build your masterpiece. Layer the fries with the cheese, charred corn, and whatever other toppings your hungry heart desires (black beans, red onion, jalapeños are all smart picks). Bake for another 5 to 7 minutes, until all that gooey cheese has melted. Remove fries from oven, dollop with some crema, and garnish with some colorful tasty things like lime wedges, cilantro, and hot sauce. Serve extra crema on the side for dipping pleasure.

FETCH FACTS

Watch where you're going, fat ass! Regina George's "fat ass" didn't actually come from her all-carb diet; Rachel McAdams wore a fat suit for the scenes where Regina had gained weight.

White Gold Hoops

For soothing your soul when Regina puts the kibosh on your favorite earrings.

Cheer up, buttercup, just because this wardrobe staple is a Plastics no-no, you can still indulge in the fried food version. These onion rings are grool! (Unless you are trying to lose three pounds.)

SERVES 4

WHAT YA NEED

- 1 large sweet onion
- 2 cups buttermilk
- About 2 cups all-purpose flour
- ¼ cup cornmeal
- 1 teaspoon baking powder
- 1½ teaspoons kosher salt, plus more to taste
- 1 cup club soda
- 1 chilled beer (Lager is best. Under 21? Ask your cool mom first.)
- 8 to 10 cups vegetable oil for frying
- Optional sauces for your dipping pleasure

SPECIAL EQUIPMENT

Candy thermometer

MAKE IT

I mean, who does Regina George think she is, telling a girl what earrings she can and can't wear!? Good news, losers, she can't ban anyone from making or *wearing* (if that's your thing) these golden delicious hoops!

- Here's how you start: Put your apron on! We are frying today, which burns like hell and will for sure ruin that cute blouse. Next, peel and carefully slice your onion into ½-inch-thick rounds. Next, soak them in a bowl of buttermilk for at least 30 minutes.

- Meanwhile, combine ¾ cup of the flour and the rest of the dry ingredients in a separate medium bowl and then pour in your club soda and lager. Whisk thoroughly so the consistency is like a thin pancake batter. A couple of lumps are okay.

- Fill a large Dutch oven or heavy bottomed saucepan with enough veggie oil to come to about a 2½-inch depth. Insert a candy thermometer and heat over medium heat until the temperature reaches 375°F. Do not cover.

- Now let's dredge and fry. Place about 1 cup flour in a separate shallow bowl. (You may need a dash more—eyeball it as you go.) Work in batches. Remove onion slices from milk, dredge in flour, and then dip into your batter. Sooo fun, right? Kinda like an assembly line!

- Now FRY. Carefully. In small batches, place your battered rings into the hot oil, watching out for splatter. Turn rings occasionally and ever so gently using tongs. Fry 'til crispy and golden. Should be less than 3 minutes.

- Line a plate with paper towels. Remove your hoops from the oil and let drain on the towels. Season with salt and serve immediately with BBQ, ketchup, ranch, or whatever sauce you fancy for your dipping pleasure! Regina can't tell you what to do now.

Spring Fling Rolls

This app is not meant to be broken in pieces and shared with the other Queens.

So, it's almost Spring Fling and ya still can't zip up the dress you reserved at 1-3-5? Munch on these rolls for the next two weeks to get zipped up and maybe even ripped up. Pick up your tray, ditch the sexually active band geeks and the Cheetos, and come on over to the Cool Asians' table because with these spring rolls on your plate, you will be a North Shore cafeteria superstar.

MAKES 6 ROLLS

WHAT YA NEED

- 1 red beet, peeled and finely grated
- ¼ cup thin strips yellow bell pepper
- ¼ cup thin strips red bell pepper
- ½ cup shredded red cabbage
- 2 carrots, sliced into thin strips
- 1 ripe mango, cubed
- 1 large bunch fresh mint, leaves only
- 1 large bunch cilantro, leaves only
- 6 rice paper spring roll wrappers
- Bonus extra protein: 8 ounces extra-firm tofu, sliced (optional)
- Lime wedges for serving
- Sauces for your dipping pleasure (optional)

MAKE IT

These rolls require some knife skills, but are fairly simple and highly satisfying! Start by prepping all of your veggies, fruits, and herbs. If you have or even know what a mandoline is, USE IT! Otherwise, pay attention and be careful with your knives beyotches: Ya don't wanna lose an acrylic before the big dance—or *worse*, in your lunch. Ewww.

- Once your ingredients are prepped, place in separate small bowls so you can form an assembly line for spring roll stuffing. Fill a large shallow dish with warm water.

- To start the assembly, dunk a rice paper wrapper in the water for 30 seconds and transfer it to a clean and slightly damp paper towel on top of a cutting board.

- Now fill your wrapper! Pretend it's the Taco Bell burrito you really want, but can't have. Get creative, use all the veggies and all the colors. Make it pretty for God's sake. Add the optional tofu if you're looking for a protein punch to the face. Roll the wrapper around the roll, tucking the ends of the wrapper in as you go, finish and seal with a little water to make ends stick. Repeat until wrappers and fillings are gone.

Serve with lime wedges and dipping sauces like store-bought ~~penis~~ **peanut** sauce, sweet chili sauce, or sriracha!

Note: Enjoy these vegan, GF, super-tasty, hope-to-make-you-skinny Spring Fling Rolls!

Cheese and Crackers for Eight People

We promise you will not feel victimized by this party spread.

This perfect platter is the pièce de résistance for throwing a massive party when your parents are away for the night. Just make sure to stash that fertility vase of the Ndebele tribe under the sink!

SERVES 8 (OR MORE)

WHAT YA NEED
Cheese and crackers
(plus other stuff)
duh

MAKE IT

A cheese plate is always a good idea. And since there is no cooking required, even the Karens in your life can handle it. Just follow these cheese platter rules and keep your fist out of your mouth:

1. Choose a variety of cheeses: **soft, semi-firm, and super-firm.** No, this is not Coach Carr's Sex Ed class notes on boner varieties, but the types of cheeses you should offer on a well-balanced cheese platter!
    - **Soft:** True crowd-pleasers are brie (maybe even baked) and Camembert.
    - **Semi-firm:** Aged Cheddar or Gruyère are great choices.
    - **Super-firm:** I personally like ~~Bradley Cooper~~; PARMIGIANO REGGIANO it's savory, slightly salty, but not too pungent. Just like Brad himself.

2. Don't forget the carbs: **Bread and crackers** are your friends. Keep it super-classy and your fertility vases hidden. A torn loaf of rustic bread mixed with a medley of crackers looks really nice and gives your refined guests a different experience with each bite.

3. Don't skimp on the accoutrements: **jams, nuts, olives, honey, dried fruit, trail mix.** I'm fairly certain if you dug through your pantry, most of you would find some, if not all of these items, so throw them on the cheese board!

4. Add some sweet stuff: **Fresh fruits,** like apples and berries, are always nice, but dried is just as good if you've got it.

5. Don't play it cool: **Serve your cheeses at room temp.** Just like no one wants a frigid date, no one wants cold cheese. Make this platter 30 minutes before your babes are supposed to roll through. It will be perfect by the time they arrive fashionably late.

6. Don't forget drinks: Have **wine & champs** on ice and ready to serve! So, you're like adulting real hard with this cheese party shindig . . . if you're gonna step up your game with a gorgeous cheese spread, don't pair it with that cheap sh*t! Buck up for a nicer bottle or at least a cheap one with a pretty label!

I Can't Help That I'm So POPular Popcorn

Ignore the haters and pass that pink popcorn.

As if you needed another reason for everyone to be so jealous of you. Your crushes will be swooning at your door every day after swim practice, begging for just one kernel of this magistical snack. Just make sure they stand on the left side waiting, because that's where they always stand.

SERVES 2 TO 4

WHAT YA NEED

- 1 (3.2-ounce) bag microwaveable popcorn (makes about 13 cups popcorn)
- 1 cup pink candy melts
- ¼ cup melted coconut oil
- 1½ cups mini marshmallows
- Pink sprinkles
- Pinch sea salt

MAKE IT

- Pop your popcorn per instructions, girl. Don't let that sh*t burn like an untreated UTI.

- Place candy melts in a microwaveable bowl and microwave 30 seconds at a time, stirring as you go, until fully melted. Thin out your melted pink goodness by adding the coconut oil. This will make this shizz drizz.

- Next, line a large baking sheet with foil and, using a metal spoon, drizzle a layer of pink candy over the foil. Lay down all the popped popcorn on top, pressing down so it sticks. Throw the marshmallows on top, mix well with your hands, and drizzle the remaining pink all over. Top with sprinkles ASAP to make sure they stick. Season with a little sea salt.

Now wait. You can check your lipstick, your Insta, and your texts, but wait . . . let this pink party cool completely before scooping into a bowl or your pie hole. Don't forget to scrape the pink chunks at the bottom, yum. If you aren't already POPular, then invite a few hungry sluts over or 'Gram this pink masterpiece and just see how many new friends/likes/followers/stalkers you'll have!

FETCH FACTS

Her hair was (actually) insured for $10,000. The wig worn by Rachel McAdams cost $10,000 as it was handmade for her by a famous wig maker in Stratford, Ontario, a famous theater town.

It's Not Regular Guac, It's Cool Guac

Your mom's favorite party dip will have nipples popping and Juicy velours dropping.

Skip today's avo toast, that's so basic. So regular mom. Let's face it, guacamole is in its prime. I know, shut up right? Perfect for happy hour (four to six daily) or an intimate after-school study sesh. This green wonder will leave you doing your sexy dance to all the coolest jams on hump day.

SERVES 2 TO 4

WHAT YA NEED

- ¼ Fuji apple
- ½ lemon
- 2 ripe avocados (duh.)
- Juice of half a lime, plus a little extra
- 2 tablespoons finely chopped sweet onion
- ¼ teaspoon salt (kosher or sea salt)
- Pinch black pepper
- 3 tablespoons pomegranate seeds
- Lime wedges to garnish
- Chips for serving

MAKE IT

Here we go. Small suggestion, you may or may not want to start with a shot of tequila...because if you're gonna drink, I'd rather you do it in the house, ya know? To get authentic and all.

- Now, get out your knives and finely chop that apple into teeny tiny pieces, to make about ⅓ cup, and place in a small bowl. Squeeze the lemon half over it, to prevent it from browning. Set aside.

- Cut your avocados in half, carefully remove the pits, and scrape your sweet, sweet avocado goodness into the nearest bowl. Add the apple, lime juice, onion, salt, and pepper. Mix until everything is mashed up with some small chunks visible. Season to taste, adding any additional salt, pepper, or a little extra lime juice you need to make it yours. Top with those pretty pomegranate seeds.

- Enjoy with lime wedges and chips, cool babes! There are no rules in this house!

FETCH FACTS

Mrs. George's dog really wanted a hump day treat of her own! A pepperoni dog treat (a Snausage) was used as Amy Poehler's nipple to get the dog to bite it and hang on.

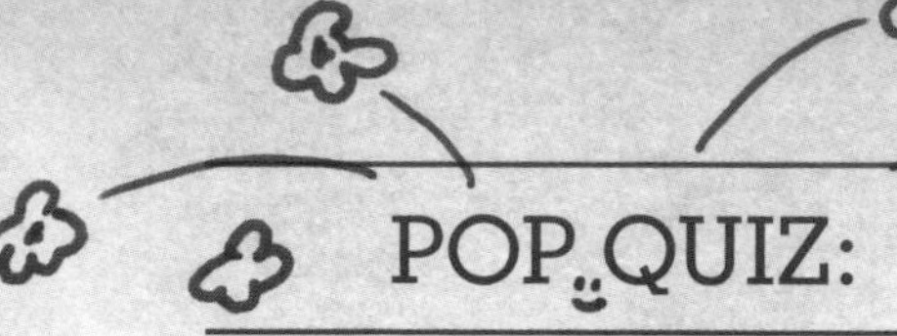

POP QUIZ:

~~LIMITS~~ WHICH PLASTIC ARE YOU?

Finding your place in the real world is hard enough, but trying to find your place in Girl World is even harder than finding someone to butter your muffin. (Even though we know Jason wants to . . . ugh, he is such a skeez.) So before we go any further, it's important to know where you rank in the army of skanks. Are you as fierce and flawless as Regina? Do you have a father cool enough to invent delicious toasted pastries? Do you just want to go back to Africa where life made sense? Or maybe you just want your pink shirt back. This quiz will tell you where you stand, or rather, who you sit with in Girl World and the recipes you'll need to master to stay there.

If you could have dinner with any person living or dead, who would you choose?

A. Paris Hilton. She might be the only person as hot as me.
B. Jane Goodall. She really knows a lot about the way things are settled in the animal kingdom.
C. Britney Spears and I could bond over the responsibilities that popularity brings.
D. I need to meet with a manicurist. My nail beds suck!
E. Danny DeVito, I love his work.
F. Winona Ryder. IDK, maybe I have a big, lesbian crush on her!

Describe your ideal date . . .

A. A fancy restaurant where I can eat my salad in a setting worthy of me.
B. A trip to the zoo.
C. Spending quality time at Barnes & Noble. I can appreciate literature!
D. Doing something fun, like playing football.
E. Dinner and a scary movie, but I have to be home by curfew!
F. Group date to the art museum.

Who is your celebrity crush?

A. I don't really have them, people just crush on me.
B. Prince Harry. He's such a worldly person.
C. Oh, Jason says I can't have celebrity crushes.
D. Al Roker and I both know when it's going to rain.
E. I'd love to do a duet with Adam Levine.
F. Billie Joe Armstrong of Green Day understands my pain and my eyeliner.

If you become Spring Fling Queen, what changes will you bring to North Shore High School?

A. This school definitely needs more mirrors.
B. I would make it so Mathletes are at the top of the food chain.
C. We need more rules, like girls should not be allowed to wear flats. I'm truly doing them a favor!
D. What is a Spring Fling, anyway? I think I had one with Seth Mosakowski.
E. We need cleaner and better-smelling men's restrooms.
F. More arts funding to get these skanks cultured.

What is the secret ingredient to make a party great?

A. Me, in a hot outfit. That's it.
B. Making sure everyone is safe and has fun.
C. Nothing matters if my man doesn't show up.
D. Twister.
E. Having snacks, including man candy.
F. First I would have to be invited to one. But I wouldn't go if the host can't be trusted.

What is your worst quality?

A. I can never choose between all the boys who love me.
B. I am too easily influenced.
C. I don't think I have one??
D. I'm failing like almost all of my classes.
E. The fact that I'm supremely under-appreciated by my classmates.
F. I get too attached to people before they inevitably betray me.

What is your best quality?

A. I am great at keeping secrets.
B. My ability to adapt, kind of like in the animal kingdom.
C. I'm like, such a good friend.
D. My talented boobs.
E. I'm truthful to women when other men won't be.
F. I'm authentic and I don't put up with anyone's sh*t.

What is your favorite home-cooked meal?

A. My mom's Cobb salad.
B. Pasta shared with my mom and dad.
C. Whatever our chef cooks.
D. Taco Bell.
E. Tacos that my nana makes, if she's not too drunk.
F. Chinese food from the mall food court.

Who is the hottest man candy at school?

A. Aaron Samuels.
B. Aaron Samuels.
C. Aaron Samuels.
D. Aaron Samuels.
E. Aaron Samuels.
F. Aaron Samuels.

What do you eat for breakfast?

A. Special K.
B. (Nor)Berries and granola.
C. Whatever Regina is having.
D. I always forget to eat breakfast, two meals is enough to remember.
E. Toaster Strudels. I like drawing pictures with the icing but I hate supporting Gretchen's dad.
F. I don't have time for that crap.

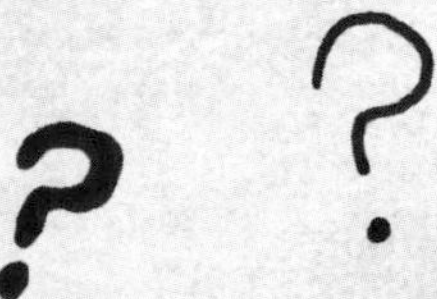

Mostly A's—Regina George

You're the Queen Bee of your friend group and you didn't get there by accident! You don't have to work at planning whores d'oeuvres for your parties, all you have to do is show up. Go to page 31 for some easy recipes that'll fit right into your all-carb diet.

Mostly B's—Cady Heron

You better stick to more laid-back functions like dinners at home with the family while listening to Ladysmith Black Mambazo because we know how your last party attempt ended. (Barf!) Turn to page 83 for some meals to help you embrace your homeschooled jungle-freak reality.

Mostly C's—Gretchen Wieners

People look to you to organize a super fetch get-together, and you have to be ready, especially if Jason shows up. It can be hard work, but you can't help it that you're popular! Turn back to page 9 and pick some snacks that'll be sure to please your guests.

Mostly D's—Karen Smith

You're the most under-appreciated member of your friend group, but where would these skanks be without you mixing up cool shooters for them? You have a lot in common with alcohol, you lighten the mood and make things fun. Go to page 119 for some drink recipes to make you drunk enough to make out with your cousin.

Mostly E's—Damian Leigh

Every Plastic needs a best gay friend — they would look like cardboard without you. Even when these train wreck bitches make a disastrous creation in the kitchen, you can make it look good with proper plating. Don't out-gay yourself, now! Look at page 137 for desserts that shine like you do.

Mostly F's—Janis Ian

These skinny boring bitches don't know sh*t about delicious food. You know there are more spices than salt and pepper and you are there to shake things up. Are you Lebanese? I feel that. Turn to page 105 for grilling recipes to throw your own pool party.

-CHAPTER 2-

Regina's All-Carb Diet

This chapter is going to make you happier than when Karen made out with her second, I mean first, cousin Seth. We've decided that the time has come to answer the question that has been on every Plastic's mind since 2004. So here it is: Is butter a carb?

Sure, Cady famously replied to Regina's legitimate question with a condescending "yes." But you dumbasses out there actually believed that homeschooled nerd? Cady was wrong. Well, mostly. As it turns out, and get ready with your muffins, ladies, butter is *not* a carb. Well it is, but it's a very low carb. Low as in it contains only 0.1 gram of carbs per stick. It's really more of a fat to be honest, but a good fat. We think?

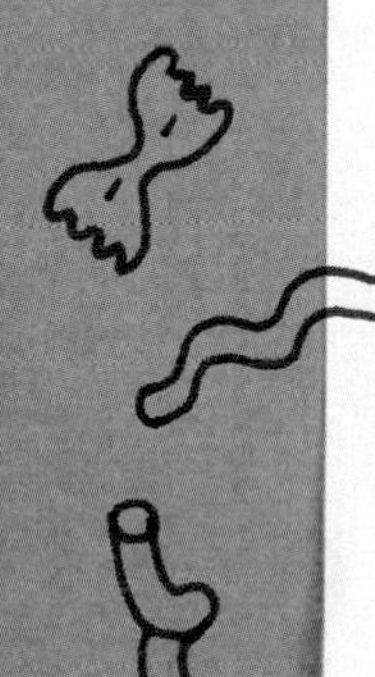

This is the best news since Danny DeVito made a cameo in the bathroom at North Shore High. It is with great pleasure that we present to you a full chapter based solely on carbs. Robert Atkins would be proud (God rest his soul). In the following pages you will find the most sinful but delightful carb recipes, including Swedish Nutrition Bars so you can go up a weight class in wrestling *or* drop all of your water weight for Spring Fling. (*Or* both? Who knows, the label is in Swedish.) We also have pasta dishes, including one where we finally make "fetch" happen and an angel hair pasta that looks so sexy pushed back you'll forget what day it is. So, start turning these pages and don't give a rat's ass what anyone says behind your back. Who cares anyways? At any second you could get hit by a bus, and then will it really matter how many thousands of carbs you inhaled at one meal? And you can always shop at Sears.

Swedish Nutrition Bars

Eat up bitch. These Swedish delights will have you looking like a regulation hottie, or high school wrestler, in no time.

Finally, the unanswered question the whole world has been waiting on—WTF are Swedish Nutrition Bars? Remember, first you bloat, then you drop ten pounds like *that*. It explains it all on the label.

MAKES 8 BARS

WHAT YA NEED

- ¼ cup rolled oats
- ½ cup protein powder
- 2 tablespoons collagen powder
- 1 cup raw cashews
- 10 large pitted dates
- ¼ cup peanut or almond butter
- 2 tablespoons honey
- Pinch sea salt
- Whole cashews or peanuts for topping (optional)
- Hemp seeds for topping (optional)

SPECIAL EQUIPMENT

Food processor

MAKE IT

- Dump your rolled oats into the food processor and pulse on low to make oat flour. Add the protein powder and collagen and blend for 30 seconds. Then slowly pulse in the cashews, dates, peanut butter, honey, and salt. Pulse on high until all the ingredients have socialized nicely. Your mix should be thick and resemble a chunky nut butter. Spread evenly in an 8x8-inch glass baking dish and pack down tightly so it's about ⅓ inch thick.

- Top with extra cashews or peanuts, maybe even hemp seeds for extra protein. Refrigerate until firm, 3 to 4 hours. Cut into bar size and enjoy cold, fresh out of the fridge.

FETCH FACTS

Jonathan would not have sat at the Varsity Jocks table in high school. He had to have a private soccer coach, who also appeared in the movie, to teach him how to score a goal on camera. It took him twenty tries to get it right! Jonathan also didn't understand why swim practice couldn't be held in the auditorium. Gawd Jonathan, you're so stupid!

Are Buttermilk Pancakes a Carb? ???

Yes. Yes they are, and they're legal in the U.S.

When you wake up from a wild Halloween party at Aaron's friend's house, this might be just what you need to make yourself feel better and soak up all those awesome shooters. Don't worry about the calories. Just don't eat anything else for the rest of the week.

SERVES 4

WHAT YA NEED

- 2 cups all-purpose flour
- 2 teaspoons baking powder
- 1 teaspoon baking soda
- ½ teaspoon pink salt
- 3 tablespoons sugar
- 2 large eggs, lightly beaten
- 3¼ cups buttermilk
- 3 tablespoons unsalted butter, melted
- Nonstick cooking spray

MAKE IT

Get your aprons and sneakers on. I mean, you don't have to have sneakers on . . . but I personally like to do calf lifts while I make pancakes to make sure the booty stays in check—knowing I'm about to carb load. #Balance

• Start by heating your griddle or skillet over medium heat. Whisk together the dry ingredients in a medium bowl: That's your flour, baking powder, baking soda, salt, and sugar, Karen. Then add in the wet ones: the eggs, buttermilk, melted butter. Combine well, but there will be lumps and that's cool. Lumps and milkshakes bring all the boys to the yard.

• Spray your hot griddle or skillet with nonstick spray. For each pancake, scoop out about ½ cup batter onto the hot griddle and cook until bubbles start to form on the top, 2 to 3 minutes. Flip and cook 'til golden. Repeat until you have a stack of pancakes filled with secrets!

Your (Angel) Hair Looks Sexy Pushed Back

How sexy do my noodles look?

You are literally going to break the internet when you post a pic of this pasta. We know everything you do is for likes anyways. But this dish is as sexy as Coach Carr. Trust us, all of your friends are going to wish they were you! Like they don't already anyways!

SERVES 6

WHAT YA NEED

- 1 pound angel hair pasta (1 box)
- 3 tablespoons olive oil, plus more for drizzling
- 2 tablespoons unsalted butter
- 4 cloves garlic, sliced
- 3 tablespoons finely chopped fresh rosemary
- Grated zest and juice of ½ lemon
- Kosher salt and freshly ground pepper to taste
- ½ cup grated Parmesan cheese
- ¼ cup chopped fresh parsley
- ¼ teaspoon chili pepper flakes, or more to taste

MAKE IT

You are looking sexy with that hair pushed back! We suggest you keep it back so you can literally dump a bowl of this pasta in your face. Yup, it's that good. Just keep it back.

- Start by cooking the pasta according to box directions, maybe minus a minute. I like pasta extra al dente, plus we're finishing it in some tasty sauce so you'll want it to soak up the extra flavor. Reserve some of the pasta water at the end—don't dump it all down the drain, like Ms. Norbury's failed marriage.

- In a large bowl, toss the drained pasta with a drizzle of olive oil and set aside.

- In a large skillet, combine the 3 tablespoons olive oil, butter, garlic, rosemary, lemon juice, and about 3 tablespoons pasta water. Bring to a simmer, making sure to not let the garlic burn. Season with salt and pepper. Throw in cooked pasta, stir to coat, and let cook for another 2 minutes or so. Then toss with the Parmesan, parsley, and chili flakes. For the extra citrus kick, top with the lemon zest and enjoy.

FETCH FACTS

Jonathan had to spend an hour with the hair department each day to have his hair flat-ironed so that it always looked sexy pushed back.

Fetch-uccini Alfredo

We're making this pasta happen, Gretchen!

We hear that in England this pasta is bigger than Toaster Strudel. But quit crying, loser, and stop trying to make garlic bread happen. This fettuccini is enough, you cow.

SERVES 5, OR 1 IF YOU'RE REALLY ON THE ALL-CARB DIET

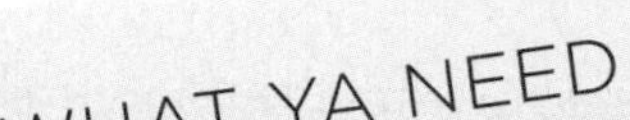

WHAT YA NEED

- 1 pound fettuccini pasta (1 box)
- 1 cup (2 sticks) unsalted butter
- 3 tablespoons heavy cream
- Pinch nutmeg
- Pinch pink salt
- ½ pound Parmesan cheese, grated

MAKE IT

FAF. Yup we said it here, this pasta is fetch as f*ck. And cheap, too, so you can keep buying those FAF Fendi purses.

- Start by cooking the pasta according to the box directions; drain, and set aside.

- In a large skillet, melt the butter over low heat and add the cream, nutmeg, and salt. Let simmer for a minute and toss in the cooked pasta and Parmesan cheese. Turn frequently to make sure the pasta gets a nice even coat of this ooey gooey sauce. Cook for an additional 2 to 4 minutes, until combined and well socialized, and serve immediately.

FETCH FACTS

We can't help it we're so popular! Even former president Barack Obama loved *Mean Girls*. The White House tweeted a picture of the first family's dog, Bo Obama, captioned "Bo, stop trying to make fetch happen."

Mac and Cheese Balls, Because I'm a Mouse, Duh

This mac and cheese is perfect for a romantic dinner with your second, I mean first, cousin Seth Mosakowski.

Incest may be frowned upon in Girl World, but this fan favorite meal could impress even your sexiest relatives. That's not right, is it? Whatever, if you'd rather sit around chowing down on comfort-carbs with your bitches while complaining about how fat you are instead,
then be our guest.

MAKES 12 BALLS

WHAT YA NEED

- 1 (7.5-ounce) box Kraft Mac and Cheese or similar (plus ¼ cup margarine and ¼ cup milk)
- 4 cups chicken broth
- 1 cup all-purpose flour
- 1 egg
- 1 cup plain breadcrumbs

Mouse Tips & Tricks: *Stir pancetta or bacon bits into the mac and cheese before pouring into the pan for a salty, meaty spin; or try garlic and parsley for an herby Italian twist.*

MAKE IT

You're a mouse, DUH! Soooo, you're obviously obsessed with cheese. Well, we've taken an easy household favorite and got a little cheffy with it so all of your li'l mouse friends will think that you belong on *Chopped* and that this cheesy delight never came from a box!

- Start the night before you want to make the balls. Make the mac and cheese according to the package instructions, but use chicken broth instead of regular water to boil the pasta, because it adds so much more flavor! Pour the mac and cheese into a 9x9-inch baking dish (or whatever you have that is close in size), cover, and let set overnight in the refrigerator.

- The next day, preheat your oven to 350°F and lightly grease a 12-cup muffin pan. Then line up three bowls on your counter. Bowl #1: Add the flour. Bowl #2: Crack in your egg and lightly beat it. Bowl #3: Add the breadcrumbs. Remove your chilled dish of mac and cheese from the fridge, scoop out a 2x2-inch piece, and use your hands to roll into a mac and cheese ball. Dredge the ball through the flour, then the egg, then the breadcrumbs. Continue this ball-making and dredging process until all the chilled mac and cheese is used up. Place the cheese balls in the muffin pan and bake for 20 to 30 minutes, until semi firm. Remove from oven and enjoy!

Oh-Snap

Is Your Cornbread Muffin Buttered?

Warning: This cornbread is so good you will want to slap us in the face. (But please don't.)

Don't be skeezed out by the name, because these wide-set muffins are big and full of secrets. No need for a bread basket that you have to share with all the other fugly and annoying people at the table, all the while pretending you don't want another one when the waiter asks. Over your bread body will you give up carbs!

MAKES 12 MUFFINS

WHAT YA NEED

- Nonstick cooking spray
- 1¼ cups all-purpose flour
- ¼ cup yellow cornmeal
- 1 tablespoon baking powder
- ½ cup sugar
- 1 teaspoon pink salt
- 2 large eggs
- 3 tablespoons honey
- ¾ cup whole milk
- ½ cup (1 stick) unsalted butter, melted and cooled
- 1 extra stick of butter to butter those muffins up!

MAKE IT

- Preheat the oven to 350°F and lightly grease a 12-cup muffin pan with nonstick spray.
- In a large bowl, whisk together your dry ingredients: the flour, cornmeal, baking powder, sugar, and salt. In a separate bowl, whisk the eggs and add the honey. Whisk again, then add the milk and whisk to combine. Slowly poor the cooled melted butter into the wet ingredients. Add the wet ingredients to the dry and stir until just blended. Do not overmix! It's okay if there are a few lumps, we promise. Spoon the batter evenly into the prepared muffin pan cups, filling each almost full. Bake for 17 to 20 minutes, until the tops are set and golden, just like last summer's spray tan. Serve warm with all the butter you can handle.

FETCH FACTS

The film was almost forced to cut the infamous "wide-set vagina" line. The MPAA wanted to give *Mean Girls* an R rating for sexual content, language, and some teen partying. It ended up being rated PG-13 but Paramount had to fight for it.

YOU GIRLS KEEP ME YOUNG

DIY Beauty

So, you agree? You think you're really pretty? If you don't, then we have a choice of masks that can help make you flawless no matter what your skin type is. Don't worry—none of them will make your face smell like a foot, but we can't help it if your face smells like peppermint or your hair like beer. Anyway, everyone at school will say: You. Look. Awesome.

Coconut ~~Foot Cream~~ Face Cream

1 tablespoon coconut oil

½ banana, mashed

Pinch turmeric

- Mix the ingredients together in a small bowl, and apply to ~~feet.~~ face Leave on for 20 minutes. Rinse with warm water. Your ~~feet~~ face will be so soft and all of the ~~fungus~~ wrinkles will magically disappear!!

Skanky Saturday Skin Detox Mask

Word vomit releases the words you were meaning to say. Actual vomit releases what your body doesn't want in it. This mask takes care of everything else. You've got to detox before you retox.

1 tablespoon witch hazel*

1 teaspoon bentonite clay

¼ teaspoon activated charcoal

½ teaspoon raw honey

- Start by mixing the witch hazel with the clay and activated charcoal in a small bowl. Then drizzle in the honey. Apply to face and leave on for 15 minutes. Rinse with warm water.

Pizza-Face Skin Clearing Mask

Keep the pizza in the cafeteria with the Varsity Jocks, not on your skin.

1 egg white

1 teaspoon lemon juice

1 teaspoon raw honey

- Whisk all ingredients together in a small bowl and apply to face. Leave on for 15 minutes. Rinse with warm water.

Spring Fling's This Weekend! Skin-Brightening Face Mask

Dress that looks amazing? Check. Hairdo that took hours? Check. What's missing is a glowing face. This easy mask will make everyone at Spring Fling say that you look really pretty tonight.

2 tablespoons Greek yogurt

1 teaspoon lemon juice

1 strawberry, mashed

- Mix all ingredients in a small bowl and apply to face. Leave on for 20 minutes. Rinse with cool water.

Full-of-Secrets Hair Volumizing Mask

Secrets are the only thing that should fill your hair and give you volume. This boozy mask will make your hair so big and beautiful you'll have to insure it for at least $10,000.

1 can beer (PBR or Coors Light are personal favs)

1 egg yolk

- Whisk your favorite beer and an egg yolk together in a small bowl. (If you tend to have dry hair or a bleached-out mane, you may wanna add 1 tablespoon of coconut oil to the mix.) Shampoo hair, towel dry, and apply hair mask. Let it soak in for 15 minutes. Rinse, shampoo again, and condition as normal.

*Note: Witch hazel is not used in Wicca, as the name suggests, so you don't need to worry about hitting up your local sketchy new-age shop. You will most likely find the witch hazel, clay, and activated charcoal at your local natural foods store. You can also buy the activated charcoal in capsules and break them open!

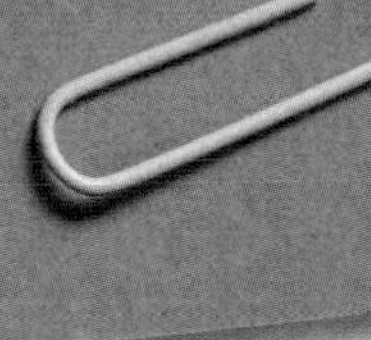

-CHAPTER 3-

I Really Want to Lose Three Pounds

Now you have come to the part of the book that we needed to include because of that obesity problem in America. Plus, you probably look like a total bushpig after going overboard with Regina's All-Carb Diet. It's time to get serious and drop the extra pounds. No need to run to the bathroom and make yourself barf (but if you do, say hi to Danny DeVito). Instead we are opting for a healthier way to get rid of the blubs.

The recipes in this chapter (jingle bell) rock! We would not disappoint you, even when it comes to the food you wouldn't wish upon a nasty army of skanks. In here, you'll find an awesome recipe for healthy-enough overnight oats (that are very grool) and a detox smoothie that will make you lose weight so quick that you will be running back to 1-3-5 for a smaller size.

For faster results, try combining these with a good amount of cardio, like swimming maybe? The swim team meets in the projection room above the auditorium for practice every week, if you're interested.

So, good luck with your new diets, bitches, and remember there's no gym for your face!

Just Stab Caesar Salad

Et tu Brute?

Just when you thought you were going to crack, along comes a Caesar salad to curb those stabby hanger pangs. No matter what Shakespeare wants us to think, Brutus was totally just as smart and cute as Caesar anyways. So, have another crouton and chill out. This dressing *is* what Rome was all about.

SERVES 2

WHAT YA NEED

FOR THE DRESSING

- 3 cloves garlic, pressed through garlic press
- 5 tablespoons olive oil (mild, not extra virgin)
- 3 tablespoons fresh squeezed lemon juice
- 2 tablespoons mayonnaise
- 2½ teaspoons Dijon mustard
- ½ teaspoon kosher salt
- 1 teaspoon freshly ground black pepper
- ¼ teaspoon Worcestershire sauce
- ½ cup grated Parmesan cheese, plus more if you want

FOR THE CROUTONS AND SALAD

- 1 nice day-old baguette
- 3 tablespoons unsalted butter
- 2 cloves garlic, minced
- Large pinch kosher salt
- 4 romaine hearts
- Freshly ground black pepper, to taste

SPECIAL EQUIPMENT

- Food processor

MAKE IT

- Start with your dressing so you give the flavors time to socialize. In the food processor, pulse your pressed garlic and then slowly drizzle in the olive oil, pulsing for another 30 seconds. Then add the lemon juice, mayo, Dijon, salt, pepper, and Worcestershire sauce and pulse again. Add the Parmesan cheese and pulse intermittently; we want to keep the dressing rustic. Pour into jar and set aside in the fridge.

- Make your croutons. Sounds intimidating, but it's super-easy and oh so fetching delicious! I like to get a nice day-old French baguette and slice it into 1-inch cubes. You'll need about 1 cup. Heat the butter in a large skillet over medium heat until melted. Add the minced garlic and toss in the bread cubes. Using tongs, coat the cubes evenly with all that garlic butter goodness. Sprinkle with your salt and continue toasting until the bread is golden and slightly crunchy. Remove from the skillet and set aside.

- Prep your romaine. You can buy pre-packed hearts or you may have to buy a few whole bunches of romaine and shed the outer leaves to get your hearts. Separate the romaine hearts into whole leaves, rinse, and pat dry thoroughly.

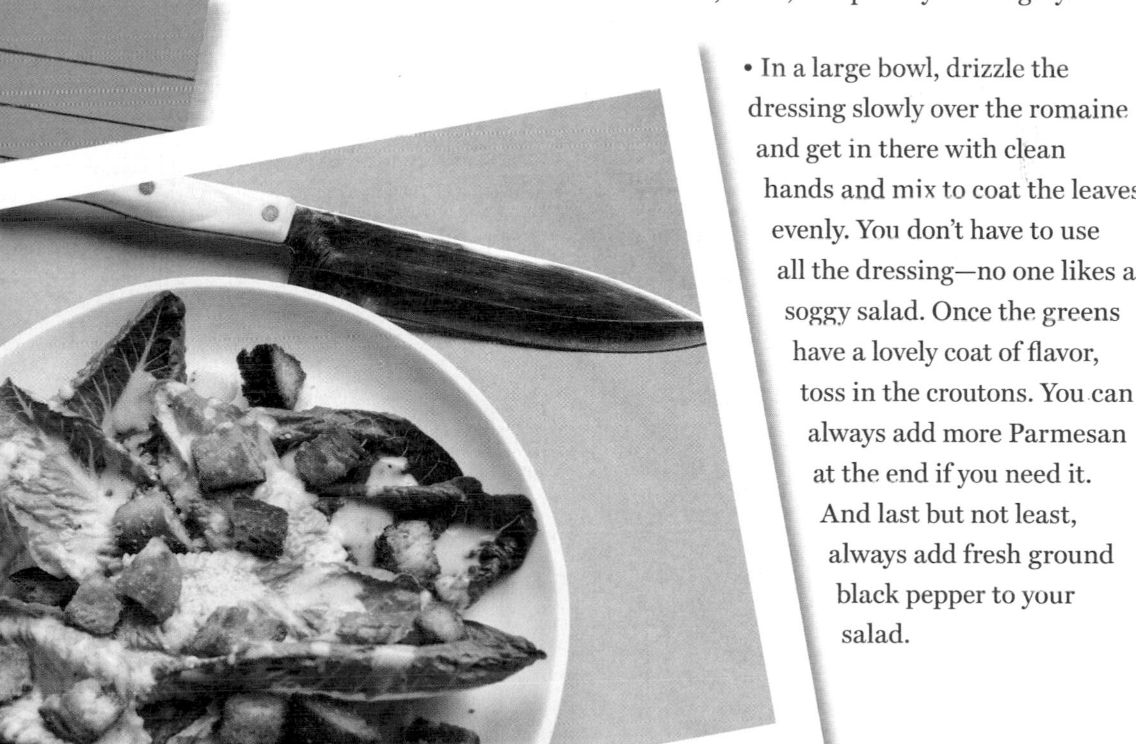

- In a large bowl, drizzle the dressing slowly over the romaine and get in there with clean hands and mix to coat the leaves evenly. You don't have to use all the dressing—no one likes a soggy salad. Once the greens have a lovely coat of flavor, toss in the croutons. You can always add more Parmesan at the end if you need it. And last but not least, always add fresh ground black pepper to your salad.

Boo You Whore-iental Salad

The salad that is there for you even when everyone else hates you.

Whether you are making out with Shane Oman or Coach Carr, or deeply involved in a four-way phone call . . . you're still a whore, boo. You didn't hear it from me though. So just eat your salad and be sad.

SERVES 2

WHAT YA NEED

FOR THE SALAD

- 2 cups chopped romaine
- 1½ cups chopped green cabbage
- 1 (11-ounce) can mandarin oranges, drained
- 4 green onions, thinly sliced
- 2 celery stalks, thinly sliced
- 1 cup honey roasted peanuts

FOR THE DRESSING

- ½ cup vegetable oil
- ¼ cup sugar
- ¼ cup white vinegar
- 1 teaspoon pink salt
- 1 teaspoon freshly ground black pepper

MAKE IT

Factorials are hard, you have to multiply each number by n, and then you get the summation. (Wrong, we are totally wrong.) But this salad is easier than Karen.

- Just mix all the salad ingredients together in a large bowl. Then mix all of the dressing ingredients together in a jar with a lid, or another sealed container, and give it a good shake. We recommend doing it in the living room, to the song "Milkshake" and swirling it over your head until you've channeled your inner Kylie George, and the dressing is good and mixed. Let sit for 10 to 15 minutes in the fridge before using; or best yet if it's made the night before. Then do what Trang Pak does best and toss that salad (with the dressing). But you don't have to use all the dressing, just toss and drizzle until your salad is coated just the way you like, and enjoy! Soggy salad is for losers!

FETCH FACTS

Damian wasn't the only one with a curfew! Since Lindsay was a minor during the shoot, her time on set was limited so her part of the four-way phone call had to be shot separately and in a higher frame rate so the director could speed it up or slow it down depending on the edit and how the dialogue would time out to match.

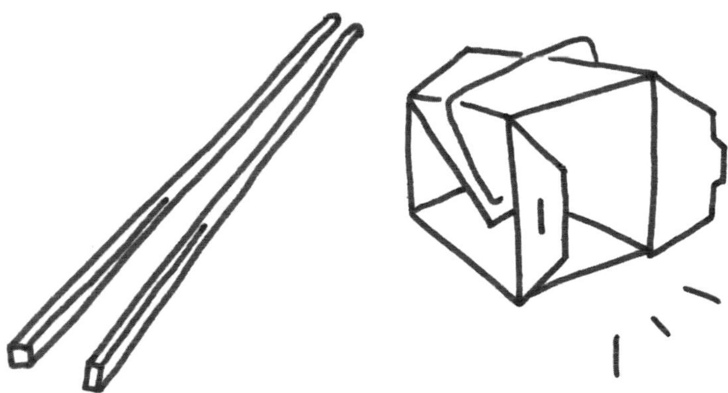

Grool Sleepover Oats

This will give you the energy you need to tell your crush what day it is.

When you wake up at a friend's house, hungover after that wild Halloween party, your body will be craving protein to help you get through the few hours of daylight you have left. Aren't you so smart you made these oats *before* you embarrassed yourself in front of your crush last night?

SERVES 2

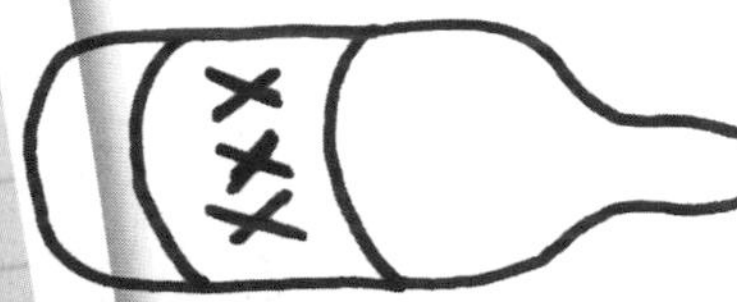

WHAT YA NEED

- ⅔ cup unsweetened coconut milk
- ⅓ cup plain Greek yogurt
- ¼ cup chopped fresh strawberries
- ½ cup rolled oats (not instant oats)
- 1½ tablespoons chia seeds
- 1 tablespoon honey
- ½ teaspoon vanilla extract
- Grated zest and juice of ½ lemon
- Pinch kosher salt

FETCH FACTS

Just like Karen asks how to spell *orange*, the internet should probably ask how to spell *grool*. It's commonly wrong online as people don't remember it's a mix between *great* and *cool*. To this day it drives Jonathan crazy when he sees it misspelled.

MAKE IT

This is some ancient *Game of Thrones* shizz. Believe it or not, *gruel* was actually a porridge served to orphans during medieval times, but the word was reincarnated when Cady got tongue-tied and combined *great* and *cool.*

- Here's what ya do: Mix all ingredients together in a cute Mason jar with tight-fitting lid. Give it a good shake and let it "sleep over" in your fridge. Enjoy in the morning straight from the jar, or scoop into a bowl and top with more fruit and seeds for that #breakfastgoals 'Gram!

Three-Days-'til-Spring Fling Cranberry Fat Flush

I know it may look like I've become a bitch, but that's only because I was dieting.

Marie Antoinette may have said, "Let them eat cake!" But we say, "Let them eat nothing!!" Remember, all you have to do is drink this for 72 hours straight and not pass out. You'll lose those three pounds like that!

SERVES 1

WHAT YA NEED

8 ounces pure cranberry juice

½ gallon alkaline water

Note: Don't actually do this "cleanse," dummies. You will die. Eat something, or at least skip to the next recipe and make a smoothie.

MAKE IT

Have no fear, the South Beach Fat Flush is here and it's so easy, your army of skanks can figure it out in their sleep. Just make sure you use 100 percent PURE cranberry juice and *not* Cranberry Juice Cocktail, which is like 1 percent juice and 99 percent sugar and belongs in the Too Gay to Function Cosmo on page 124.

- Mix your juice and water and drink this, and nothing but this. Repeat as needed for 72 hours.

FETCH FACTS

Why are you so obsessed with me? Lindsay Lohan auditioned for the role of Regina George and Rachel McAdams auditioned for Cady Heron.

You Smell Like a Baby Prosti-turmeric Latte

No honey, pumpkin spice lattes are yesterday's news.

SERVES 2

WHAT YA NEED

1 (13.5-ounce) can coconut milk
1 cup almond milk
15 to 20 saffron threads
4 whole black peppercorns
1 teaspoon ground turmeric
1 teaspoon rose water, plus a little extra
1 tablespoon honey
1 teaspoon vanilla extract

MAKE IT

- In a small saucepan over low heat, bring the coconut and almond milk to a gentle simmer. Slowly add in the remaining ingredients, while stirring constantly. Let the flavors socialize for about 5 to 7 minutes. Make sure to not burn the milks!

- Pour the liquid through a fine mesh strainer and into two mugs. Garnish with a pinch of cinnamon and serve immediately. Splash some of the extra rose water on your face to smell extra fresh and floral you dirty whore.

Namaste, beyotches.

You Will Get Pregnant and Diet Smoothie

This is for when your sweatpants are all that fit you right now.

Too bad you skipped that first day of health class. Fruits and veggies are for more than putting rubbers on. Think of it this way, you could keep yelling at your bitchy best friend for posting unflattering pics of you on the 'Gram, or you could shut up and start guzzling. This smoothie will have you running faster than Coach Carr chasing minors. See you in Sex Ed!

MAKES 1 SMOOTHIE

WHAT YA NEED

- 1 cup frozen raspberries
- 1 ripe banana, sliced
- 1 big handful spinach and/or kale
- 6 ounces unsweetened almond milk
- 2 tablespoons organic flax oil
- 2 tablespoons organic virgin coconut oil
- 1 tablespoon honey

Super-Healthy Note: Add a scoop of protein powder for extra health benefits, and try to use only organic fruits and veggies whenever possible.

MAKE IT

- Step 1: Place all the above ingredients in blender and blend until smooth.
- Step 2: Enjoy eating clean for once, you dirty whore.

FETCH FACT

Dirty birdy Coach Carr, who in the movie taught health class before getting caught with Trang Pak in the projection room above the auditorium, was played by Dwayne Hill, who has been nominated for an Emmy for his work as a voice over performer.

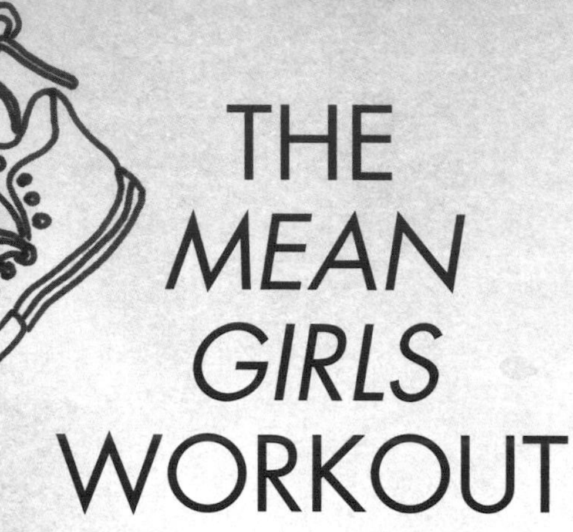

THE *MEAN GIRLS* WORKOUT

How bad do you wanna lose those three pounds?

Contrary to popular belief, Swedish Nutrition Bars do *not* help you lose weight. Then again neither does stuffing your face with Gretchen's Wieners or chugging our Frosé by the gallon, but ya still did that. So now you've got some work to do. It's time to turn on the movie, yes, we know you just watched it. But don't be a skank whore and act like you're not gonna just watch it again anyway. (Ugh, why are you so obsessed with us?) It's time to turn you mean girls into lean girls by following along with the movie and the workout instructions below. If you truly want to sit with us, then you are going to have to bite the bullet and sweat with us. On Wednesdays we wear pink, but every day we work out and turn pink.

Are you wondering how many times you should do this workout to obtain a perfect body? The answer is simple: The limit does not exist! So, take a lesson from Regina's little sister Kylie, a Plastic in training, and push those coffee tables to the side of the room, throw your arms above your head, and move your bodies until you sweat like Coach Carr did when he got caught sucking face with Trang Pak.

KICK BUTT!

10 jumping jacks	Whenever someone says *fetch*
15 squats	Whenever someone says *slut*
10 sit-ups	Whenever someone says *Mathletes*
Jog in place	Whenever the burn book is open. Keep moving the *whole* time it is open.
Lunge in place	During any African montage
Burpees nonstop	For duration of the Halloween party
20 butt kicks	For every on-screen kiss
15 high knees	Whenever someone mispronounces *Cady*
5 push-ups	For each time you hear *shut up*
Hold a plank	When the Mathlete competition is on screen
10 bicycle twists	Whenever Aaron tries to do math

*******For extra cardio do the entire dance to "Jingle Bell Rock," but make sure you stand to the left and watch out for flying boom boxes.*

Now raise your hands if you feel personally victimized by this work out. You can thank us later.

-CHAPTER 4-

On Wednesdays We Eat, Drink, and Wear Pink

Let's go over the rules for being a Plastic:

1. We never wear a tank top two days in a row.
2. We only wear our hair in a ponytail once a week.
3. We only wear jeans or track pants on Fridays.
4. We always vote when we want to ask someone to eat lunch with us, because you have to be considerate of the rest of the group.
5. On Wednesdays, we wear pink!

Do you get the drift? Wednesdays are all pink all the time, so you'd best get with it or you'll be sitting alone again in the ladies' room again with your sad stall salad.

Give these hump-day recipes a go and you'll be pretty in pink in no time. Our Strawberry Frosé is the bomb. Even Damian's nana goes wild over it. Just make sure she keeps her wig on. The Strawberry Frosé (page 74) is perfect for washing down that Beet Hummus (page 70). (Both so good that you're going to have urges to take off your clothes and touch each other! But don't because then you will get chlamydia and die.)

If you truly want in with this scum-sucking road whore crowd (which you do, obvs) then borrow the nearest pink shirt and get cooking. We know you can't help it that you're so popular.

I Want My Pink Soup Back! Watermelon Gazpacho

Never trust a Plastic with your favorite clothes.

Oh, hey hottie! This chilled summer treat will help you keep your cool after a total meltdown. It's low in calories, highly tasty, and Wednesday Pink approved. Regina swears it's only 120 calories and 48 calories from fat (if you garnish with avocado).

SERVES 4

WHAT YA NEED

- 7 cups chopped watermelon
- 3 small to medium tomatoes, chopped
- ¼ cup fresh mint leaves, plus more for garnish
- 1 teaspoon fresh lime juice
- 1 teaspoon agave nectar
- 2½ teaspoons pink salt
- ½ cup crumbled feta
- Diced avocado for garnish (optional)

SPECIAL EQUIPMENT

- Food processor

FETCH FACTS

Lindsay Lohan was *cough cough* sick with a case of PINK eye when they shot the scene with Aaron Samuels asking to borrow a pencil in math class. Good thing her stand-in, Michelle Hoffman, had her back.

MAKE IT

- Place 6 cups of the watermelon, the tomatoes, mint, lime juice, agave, and salt in the food processor and pulse. You'll want a rustic, slightly chunky texture, so don't overprocess. Pour into a storage bowl with a lid and stir in the final cup of watermelon chunks. Cover and chill for at least half an hour before serving.

- When ready to serve, divide chilled soup among four bowls and garnish with feta, mint, and avocado. Eat immediately.

She's Fabulous, but She's Evil. And These Are Her Deviled Eggs.

These deviled eggs are life ruiners!

So, you've never seen pink eggs before? Are you on crack? You are just so lucky you have us to guide you. Just remember, we know your secret—Planned Parenthood called and your test results are in.

MAKES 12 EGGS

WHAT YA NEED

- 6 large eggs
- 1 (16-ounce) can pickled beets
- 1 cup apple cider vinegar
- ⅓ cup packed brown sugar
- 1 teaspoon pink salt
- 1 tablespoon black peppercorns
- 2 tablespoons olive oil
- 1 tablespoon mayonnaise
- 1 tablespoon white distilled vinegar
- 1 teaspoon Dijon mustard
- Kosher salt and freshly ground black pepper to taste
- Fresh herbs for garnish

SPECIAL EQUIPMENT

- Pastry bag (or large ziplock bag)

DIY Beauty Note: Beet juice can be used as a naturally organic lip or cheek stain! Use some of the extra juice from this recipe to make your face pretty! Please, don't be a fugly hostess.

MAKE IT

- In a medium saucepan, add eggs and cover with room temperature water. Turn heat to high and bring to boil. Once boiling, set timer for 7 to 8 minutes. Immediately remove from heat and rinse with cool water. Let eggs drain and cool completely. Peel shells and set the eggs aside.

- To make the brine for pickling, drain the beets in a mesh strainer over a bowl, then transfer the beet juice to a large Mason jar (or any container with a tight-fitting lid). Add the cider vinegar, brown sugar, pink salt, and peppercorns and stir to combine. Add the hard-boiled eggs to the brine and stir gently. All the eggs should be fully submerged. Cover and chill for at least 12 hours. (The longer you leave your eggs in the brine, the darker pink they will become, so be patient.)

- When the eggs have reached prime pink-ness, drain. Slice each in half and transfer the yolks to a medium bowl. Add the olive oil, mayo, white vinegar, and mustard and mash 'til smooth and creamy. Pipe the mixture back into the egg halves using a pastry bag; or, you can hack it with a ziplock with a corner snipped off. Sprinkle with salt and pepper and garnish with herbs.

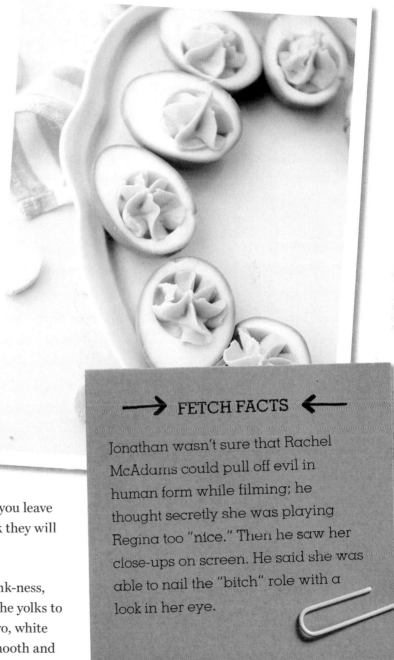

→ FETCH FACTS ←

Jonathan wasn't sure that Rachel McAdams could pull off evil in human form while filming; he thought secretly she was playing Regina too "nice." Then he saw her close-ups on screen. He said she was able to nail the "bitch" role with a look in her eye.

Burn Brunch Citrus Salad

If you can't spell O-R-A-N-G-E by now, then you should probably burn this book.

When life gives you lemons, oranges, and grapefruit . . . make an effing salad! OMG. This salad is sooooo pretty and perfect for a bitchy #burnbrunch fest with your ladies. And it's *loaded* with vitamin C, which I heard might even cure an STD or whatever.

SERVES 4

WHAT YA NEED

FOR THE SALAD

- 2 mandarin oranges
- 2 medium oranges
- 2 ruby red grapefruits
- Torn fresh basil and mint for garnish

FOR THE DRESSING

- Juice of 3 limes
- Juice of 1 lemon
- 3 tablespoons honey
- ¼ cup olive oil
- Dash pink salt (duh)

MAKE IT

- This dish is so easy, even a homeschooled jungle freak could make it. Start by peeling your citrus fruits and cutting away any of the nasty bitter white pith on the outsides. Slice the citrus into uniform ¼-inch-thick rounds. Arrange the rounds on a pretty platter.
- Next, mix all of your dressing ingredients in a jar. Drizzle on the salad, garnish with herbs of your choice, and eat up!

De-Lish

I'm Sorry People Are So Jealous of My Perfect Pink Taco

Open those wide-set jaws and start eating.

Eating these tacos is like being famous. You can eat them while wearing army pants and flip flops, or after canoodling with bae at the Halloween party. We should know, we like invited them, you know?

MAKES 6 TACOS

WHAT YA NEED

- 1 medium red onion
- Juice of 2 limes, plus wedges for serving
- ¾ teaspoon pink salt
- ¾ cup mayonnaise
- ¾ cup fresh cilantro leaves
- ½ teaspoon ground cumin
- 1 pound medium shrimp, peeled, deveined, and tails removed
- 1 cup shredded coleslaw mix (store-bought is fine)
- 1 small jalapeño, seeded and diced
- 6 corn tortillas

SPECIAL EQUIPMENT
Food processor

MAKE IT

- Preheat your oven to 375°F. We're gonna start by pickling our onion. It's Wednesday and we want them to be pink, so it's essential you use a red onion. Peel that onion and slice thinly, preferably using a mandoline if you have one. Place the onion slices in a small bowl along with half of the lime juice and a pinch of salt. Set aside, stirring every so often.

- In the food processor, combine the mayo, cilantro, ground cumin, and remaining lime juice. This sauce is key, it marinates your shrimp and dresses your coleslaw. Place your cleaned shrimp in a medium bowl and add half of the mayo mixture. Let them all marinate or socialize—which is what I like to think ingredients do—for a solid 15 minutes.

- In a medium bowl, mix the rest of the mayo mix with the shredded coleslaw, toss with diced jalpeños for a little kick and set aside.

- To cook the shrimp: Wrap them all in a foil pouch and bake on the middle rack for 7 to 9 minutes. Shrimp is a great protein to try out, even if you're a rookie chef . . . it changes color when it's done and it won't kill you if it's under- or overcooked!

- Remove the shrimp from the packet. Assemble your tacos by layering each corn tortilla with shrimp, coleslaw, and pickled onion. Garnish with lime wedges and cilantro. Serve with tequila and a curious open mind. I mean it doesn't count if you only ate it once back in college. Right?

Give Me a Beet Hummus

Take it from Kevin G., and don't let the haters stop you from doing your thang!

All . . . you . . . sucka emcees ain't got beets like me. Wednesdays call for hummus with some flavor. Rock that varsity jacket and share the beets with yo 'letes, but don't be a double dipper, you nasty skank.

SERVES 8 TO 10

WHAT YA NEED

- 2 small beets, trimmed and scrubbed
- Olive oil for drizzling
- 2 (12-ounce) cans no-salt-added chickpeas, drained and rinsed
- ⅓ cup tahini
- ¼ cup lemon juice
- 2 cloves garlic, chopped
- ¼ teaspoon sea salt
- 1 tablespoon hemp seeds for garnish
- Variety of veggies for dipping
- Toasted pita bread for dipping

SPECIAL EQUIPMENT

Food processor or blender

FETCH FACT

A line cut from Kevin G.'s rap was, "It ain't no trick / I am this slick / All the ninth-grade ladies / Wanna suck my—WHAT!"

(((MAKE IT)))

- Start by cooking your beets. Preheat the oven to 425°F. Drizzle the beets with olive oil and wrap each in foil. Bake for 45 to 55 minutes, until fork tender. Remove the beets from oven and unwrap—careful, they will be hot! Place under cool running water and remove the skins. Slice into ¼-inch chunks.

- In the food processor or blender, combine the cooked beets, chickpeas, tahini, lemon juice, garlic, and sea salt and blend 'til smooth, about a minute or so. Transfer pink hummus to a serving dish and garnish with a swirl of olive oil and hemp seeds if you've got them. Serve with cut-up veggies and pita for your dipping party pleasure!

Queen Beet-za

Bow down bitches, there is a new Queen Bee in town and she's bringing this pizza.

Raise your hand if you have been personally victimized by the pizza delivery guy? This take on pizza is like practically a vegetable, such a great shade of pink, and so easy to make at home you barely need to get off your fat ass to do it. Word on the street is that Regina George brought this pizza to-go on a plane and John Stamos told her he thought it was pretty. So, there's that.

SERVES 4

SPECIAL EQUIPMENT
Food processor, rolling pin (or see Note)

WHAT YA NEED

FOR THE PIZZA

- 6 medium-small beets, trimmed and scrubbed
- 4 cloves garlic, peeled
- 1 tablespoon olive oil, plus more for drizzling
- 1 tablespoon tomato paste
- 1 tablespoon balsamic vinegar
- Kosher salt to taste
- Handful of all-purpose flour
- 1 (16-ounce package) store-bought pizza dough (Trader Joe's has whole wheat dough!)
- 8 ounces soft ricotta cheese

PRETTY AF TOPPINGS

- Arugula
- Fresh parsley or rosemary
- Thinly sliced candy cane beets (pictured, these beauties are seasonal)

- Get your oven on to 425°F. In a medium pot of salted water, bring beets to a boil and cook for 15 to 20 minutes, until fork tender. Rinse beets and slice into quarters. In the food processor, combine the beets, garlic, olive oil, tomato paste, vinegar, and salt. Pulse until all ingredients are well blended and smooth, 3 to 5 minutes. Set the beet sauce aside.

Mean Girls was based on the book *Queen Bees and Wannabes* by Rosalind Wiseman.

- Next, find a large clean surface in your kitchen. (Think cutting board or smooth countertop. Or, if you're a loser and don't have a big cutting board, you can use two paper grocery bags that have been opened up and laid flat on the counter—easy and disposable cleanup bonus!) Lightly dust the surface with some flour and begin to roll out your dough with the rolling pin. Roll the dough out into a thin circle that is 8 to 10 inches in diameter. Place the dough round on a baking sheet and drizzle lightly with olive oil. Bake according to package instructions for about 10 minutes, until golden in color. Remove crust from oven.

- Spread the beet sauce evenly over the crust, and drop 1-inch clumps of ricotta on top. Bake for another 10 minutes, so the cheese can get nice and gooey. Remove from the oven.

- We like to add the fresh green toppings at the end so you have a nice mix of cooked and raw textures. This little touch gives the Beet-za an almost healthy-ish feel.

Note: Not much of a baker? Don't have a rolling pin, but happen to be a lush? AWESOME! An empty wine bottle with the label removed works just as well as a rolling pin. Make sure to lightly dust it with flour and you're good to go! Insert "Rollin' with the homies" GIF here.

Strawberry Frosé, Obvi

Drink this on Wednesdays . . . and Thursdays . . . and Saturdays . . .

When all you want to do is come home and pour yourself some dinner, this is the perfect meal replacement. This frosé can also be enjoyed while sitting around your swimming pool with your besties (or the ones pretending they're your besties) and writing down everything you hate about everyone else. This is also a great way to get in your daily intake of water.

SERVES 6 (UNLESS YOU'RE A LUSH, THEN SERVES 1)

WHAT YA NEED

1 (750-milliliter) bottle rosé wine
1 additional 750 milliliter bottle rosé wine
½ cup water
½ cup sugar
1 pound strawberries, hulls removed

SPECIAL EQUIPMENT
Blender

MAKE IT

First things first, put on "Roses" by the Chainsmokers. It was *the* song of summer for 2015. The same summer frosé became a thing. Talk about the universe lining up on that one! #Blessed

- Okay, open your wine bottles to let the rosé breathe, then load up your blender with the water, sugar, and strawberries. Blend 'til smooth. While blending, grab a glass and pour yourself some juice, and by juice, I mean the pink grape stuff. Sip, shoot, chug, whatevs, and get back to work.

- Pour the strawberry mixture into a baking dish and add only 1 bottle of wine. The other bottle is to make sure you stay hydrated while making this, duh. Place the baking dish in freezer on a flat surface. Go back to your other wine bottle and enjoy . . . for about 2½ hours. Now you should stir your frosé with a fork, so it's slushy. Then resume drinking, freezing, and dancing to the Chainsmokers . . . *Say you'll never let me go . . .*

- After 5 hours, countless selfies, and more than half of your day (but trust me, this shizz is worth it), remove the baking dish from freezer and give it a good stir to break up any big ice chunks. Serve immediately in super-cute dessert cups.

'Gram Note: Top your frosé with edible flower. Serve with rose gold spoon. (I mean, how could you not?) Snap a pic and tag #TheBurnCookBook #PlasticsLoveFrose #OnWednesdaysWeDrinkPink

HEY → Not Word Salad. Actual Pink Salad.

Not Word Salad. Actual Pink Salad.

OMG, are pink greens still greens? Can you even ask that?

True story: Nikki discovered a gorgeous pink leafy veggie while on a late night store run after a *Yes way Rosé* type Saturday: *pink radicchio*, hidden among the Cheetos! Dreams do come true! So, she did what any chef girl would do and grabbed it, then went home to make the prettiest damn salad that anyone ever saw—at 3 a.m.! And then ate the Cheetos. Because let's be real, no salad prevents a hangover, no matter how pretty it might be.

SERVES 6

WHAT YA NEED

FOR THE SALAD

- 2 heads pink radicchio
- 1 head pink napa cabbage
- 2 small candy cane beets, trimmed, peeled, and thinly sliced
- 1 bunch multi-colored radishes cut in quarters
- ½ cup thinly sliced fennel
- 1 cup red raspberries

FOR THE CITRUS CHAMPAGNE VINAIGRETTE

- ½ cup extra virgin olive oil
- ½ cup fresh orange juice
- 3 tablespoons champagne vinegar
- 1 tablespoon honey
- Kosher salt to taste

FETCH FACTS

It turns out that word *vomit* is acceptable in a PG-13 movie, but actual vomit is not. In the party scene where Cady pukes on Aaron Samuels, Jonathan had the props team make the vomit out of chicken soup and Cheerios hurled onto his lap. He was later disappointed that the audience didn't get to see his masterpiece on camera.

MAKE IT

Okay, so here's what ya need to do. It's a salad, so get creative with your assembly and plating. We prefer salads on large, shallow platters—rather than deep bowls—so you can really get a visual of what's in them. Make sure your veggies have been washed and dried thoroughly. A caterpillar in your pretty salad will absolutely ruin brunch. Butterflies are pretty. Caterpillars are furry and can be terrifying.

- Trim the heads and stems of the radicchio and cabbage, then tear into manageable pieces (do not cut these gorgeous lettuces, we're going farm-to-table here). Scatter them on the platter and layer on the sliced beets, radishes, fennel, and raspberries.

- For the dressing, mix all ingredients in a large Mason jar. If ya have a lid, give it a good shake, otherwise whisk 'til all ingredients are well socialized. Drizzle over the salad and enjoy! For extra credit: Garnish your sald with fresh herbs like mint, dill, or parsley.

Do Not Trust These Treats

Don't be a skank, make enough for everyone who goes here.

Warning: These gooey bars are so good, you may just find yourself bingeing on them in a dark corner in the projection room, above the auditorium. But remember to share with the rest of the lacrosse team, or you deserve to get hit by a bus.

MAKES 24 TREATS

WHAT YA NEED

¼ cup (½ stick) unsalted butter

1 (10½-ounce) bag mini marshmallows

8 cups Very Berry Cheerios

Pink sprinkles (optional)

MAKE IT

- Start by melting your butter in a large saucepan or Dutch oven over low to medium heat. Add the marshmallows and stir until melted. Next, slowly add the Cheerios, a little at a time, while stirring and coating them. Make sure all the Cheerios are nice and coated in the marshmallow mixture before adding another scoop. Continue until you've added all the cereal.

- Pour the mixture into a 9x13-inch pan greased with butter, carefully packing the mixture down evenly. Allow to cool. Top with pink sprinkles and unicorn dust. Slice into 2x2-inch squares, 4x4 if you're a fatty.

MEAN GIRLS MASH

Karen's boobs can tell when it's raining, but they can't tell the future! That's where this game comes in. This *Mean Girls* version of MASH will tell you exactly what will happen to you, good or bad. As Cady said before a very unfortunate barfing incident: I would never lie to you. Good luck! *kiss kiss*

How to play: Remember life before cell phones? MASH and Britney Spears were like all we had in 2004. MASH stands for Mansion, Apartment, Shack, House—i.e., your future abode—and no Plastic wants to live in a shack, so don't F this up.

Ask a friend to draw a spiral on a sheet of paper until you tell her to stop! Draw a line through it and count the rings. Like this:

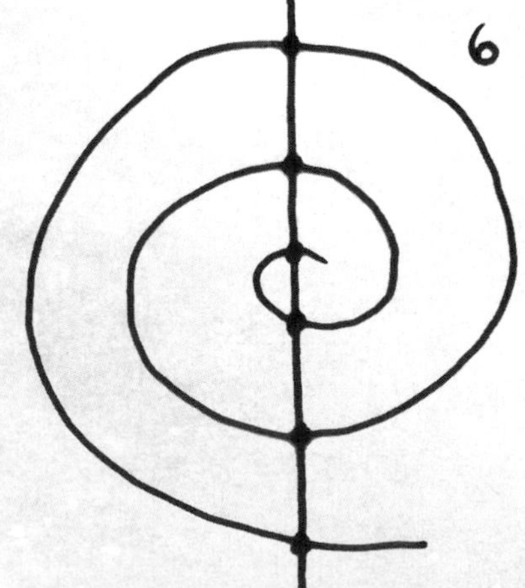

Remember that number. Say, for example, the number is six. Go down our MASH board and cross off every sixth thing, remembering to skip the section headings. On our board you would cross out "Regina," then "Shane," then "School Bus," then "Mouse"... you get the idea. Every sixth thing bites the dust. Keep crossing off names, places, etc. until you are down to one answer in each category. Circle that bitch! That's your future!

MASH

Career

Research zoologist

Schoolteacher

Bartender at T.J. Calamity's

Babysitter

Inventor

Bestie

Regina

Cady

Gretchen

Karen

Janis

Man Candy

Aaron

Shane

Jason

Damian

Kevin G.

Ride

You can walk home, bitch!

Silver Lexus

School bus

Escalade

Ford Taurus with a sun roof

Pet

Chihuahua

Dog that can walk on its hind legs

Bunny

Mouse

Cat

Number of Children

1

2

3

4

5

Where You Will Live

Africa

Evanston, Illinois

Michigan

Rome

Lebanon

-CHAPTER 5-

Cramming for Finals

It's that time of the year again: finals. If you've spent most of the year trying to be a life-ruiner like Regina, then you've most likely left all your studying to the last minute. You should have asked that regulation hottie in math class to be your tutor back on October 3rd. But once again, we're here to rescue you with brain food even Ms. Norbury would approve of.

These are serious meals to keep you studying . . . we don't care how long it takes. We will keep you here all night if we have to. Or at least until four. Our recipe for Swedish Meatballs (page 98) is sure to give you a boost of energy. That's what protein does right? Whatever, we're getting cheese fries. But seriously we'll bet you a gift certificate to IHOP that you'll get at least three hundred likes on your Insta pic of our Orange Chicken (page 92). Do you even know how to spell *orange*? We are already predicting that our recipe for the Total Meltdown toasts (page 90) will be a fan favorite. You'll have to make them for all your study buddies (how else will you get them to give you their notes from all the classes that you were too *cough cough* sick to go to). There's a 30 percent chance you will pass.

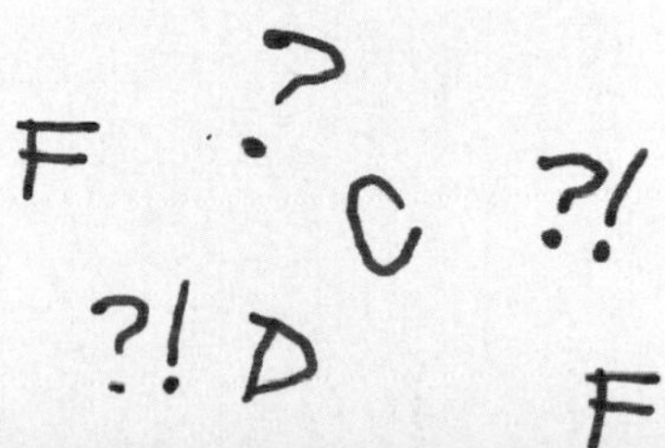

Aaron Samuels's Actual Mom's Chicken Stuffed Shells

To be enjoyed and savored with the people you love.

ACTUAL HUMAN BEING ALERT—A note from Jonathan:

SERVES 6 TO 8

One thing that I related to playing Aaron Samuels is that he definitely cares about school, his mom, and his friends . . . a lot. It was important to me to keep my mom's legacy alive. One way of doing this was to share with you the most famous of all of her recipes: these cheesy gooey shells. They were such a staple in my childhood and brought our neighborhood together and have that comforting touch. When Regina brings the Plastics home after school and Mrs. George asks them if they're hungry, well . . . the same thing happened at the real Bennett house every day. It was everyone's home away from home. However, instead of serving a hump day treat, Ruthanne Bennett would serve her famous Chicken Stuffed Shells. So get ready: You're about to make something you will become even more obsessed with than yourselves. And in the spirit of Mrs. Bennett, the OG Mrs. Samuels, make sure you make more than enough to share, because these little cups of chicken and stuffing are meant to bring people together.

Be happy!

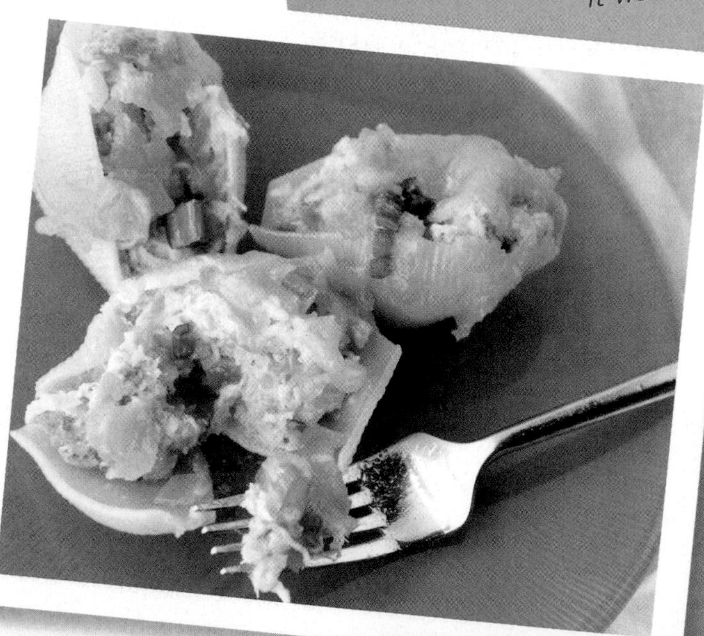

WHAT YA NEED

1 (12-ounce) box jumbo pasta shells
1 (10-ounce) box chicken-flavored stuffing mix
2 boneless skinless chicken breasts
½ cup mayonnaise
2 (10¾-ounce) cans cream of chicken soup
1 cup water
1½ cups shredded Cheddar cheese
Nonstick cooking spray
¼ cup chopped scallions for garnish

MAKE IT

The key to this comfort food is comfort. It should be made with your best girlfriends, in the comfy sweatpants that still fit you, while you all talk about the latest total beyotch and put them in the burn book.

- Preheat your oven to 350°F.

- Cook the shells per the package instructions until al dente. Make sure to salt the cooking water. Drain and set aside.

- Make the stuffing per the package; set aside to let cool.

- Bring a medium saucepan of water to a boil. Add the chicken, reduce to a simmer over medium heat, and poach for 16 to 18 minutes, or until breasts are cooked through and have an internal temperature of 165°F. Drain and cool on a cutting board. Cut into small pieces or shred with two forks.

- In a large bowl, mix the chicken with the mayo, then fold in the stuffing.

- In another medium bowl, combine the soup and water to thin. Spoon a small amount into a 9x12-inch baking dish and spread to cover the bottom. (If you don't, your shells will stick and fall apart, just like all of your relationships.)

- Stuff the cooked pasta shells with the chicken mixture and place in your prepared baking dish. You don't want to overload these little boats of comfort too much, they should look like individuals in the pan—not like some sea of Junior girls with attitude problems. Spoon the remaining soup over the shells, and top with the cheese. Coat a piece of aluminum foil with nonstick cooking spray and cover the baking dish tightly. Bake for 35 to 45 minutes. Remove foil and return to the oven for another 5 to 10 minutes so the cheese melts to an ooooey gooey golden glaze. Garnish with chopped scallions when you're ready to serve or stuff your face!

Save Your Fresh Mani Kitchen Hack: Place your poached chicken breasts in a food processor with the paddle attachment and let the shredding begin! Just don't overmix or it will be chicken mush. I love my SMEG processor, it's PINK and has a cute retro look!

JAMBO-laya

My fifth sense tells me you'll like it extra spicy.

Say "hello"—I mean "Jambo!"—with this spicy dish and you will have every mean girl in the school speaking Swahili (or Swedish?) in no time! Trust us. We don't need to have ESPN to predict it.

SERVES 6 TO 8

WHAT YA NEED

- 2 tablespoons olive oil
- 2 tablespoons butter
- 1 pound boneless, skinless chicken breasts, cut into bite-size pieces
- 3 andouille sausage links, sliced
- 1 cup chopped sweet onion
- ½ cup bite-size pieces yellow bell pepper
- ½ cup bite-size pieces green bell pepper
- 1 cup chopped celery
- 1 jalapeño, seeded and diced
- 5 cloves garlic, chopped
- 1 (8-ounce) can tomato puree
- ½ cup chicken broth
- 2 tablespoons Cajun or Creole seasoning

HA-CHA-CHA!!!

- Pinch pink salt
- ¼ teaspoon ground black pepper
- 1 dried bay leaf
- 1½ cups white rice, cooked
- 1 pound medium shrimp, shelled and deveined
- Chopped fresh chives and parsley for garnish
- Grilled French bread for serving
- 1 lemon, cut into wedges, for serving
- Hot sauce for serving (optional)

MAKE IT

- In a large stockpot, heat the olive oil and butter over medium heat. Add the chicken and sausage and cook for 5 to 7 minutes, until golden brown, turning once or twice. Add the onion, bell peppers, celery, jalapeño, and garlic and cook until the onion is translucent and the garlic becomes aromatic. Add the tomato puree, broth, seasoning, salt, pepper, and bay leaf. Simmer over low heat for 20 minutes. Add the cooked rice and shrimp and continue simmering for 10 minutes, until the shrimp is cooked through. Remove the bay leaf and ladle the jambalaya into bowls.

- Garnish with chives and parsley and serve with grilled bread and lemon wedges. Have hot sauce on deck if you like it extra spicy!

FETCH FACT

Goodbye Abercrombie & Fitch, hello high school. When Jonathan was cast as Aaron Samuels, he said goodbye to his job as a greeter at Abercrombie & Fitch and "Jambo!" to the *Mean Girls* set. Originally, someone else was cast to play Aaron Samuels, but after a last-minute creative decision, the other actor was let go and producers said, "Get in, loser, we're going shopping." Jonathan jumped on a plane to Toronto to start filming the next day.

Total Meltdown

Warning: Devouring these in public may cause social suicide.

Here are the steps to eating these cheesy toasts and feeling like a real Plastic:

Step 1. Eat in private. Like in the bathroom or something at lunchtime.

Step 2. Cry. Just let it flow.

MAKES 24 TOASTS

WHAT YA NEED

- 6 tablespoons (¾ stick) unsalted butter
- 1 French baguette
- 3 tablespoons all-purpose flour
- ⅓ cup whole milk
- 5 ounces Gruyère cheese, shredded
- ½ cup cooked diced pancetta
- Pinch fresh nutmeg
- Pink salt and freshly ground pepper to taste

FETCH FACTS

If Janis had a wig, it could have been made of the lunch lady's chest hair! One of the assistant directors, Joel Hay, dressed up as a woman to play a cafeteria lady at the checkout line.

LOL

MAKE IT

Nominated for Queen or not, this cheesy gooey snack gets all the votes at North Shore High! Seriously, when you might be losing your sh*t, the only way to pull it back together is with a solid dose of cheese and ham. This gooey delight should do the trick for all the girls who like to eat their feelings.

- Preheat your oven to 375°F. Melt 3 tablespoons of the butter in a medium saucepan. Slice your baguette lengthwise in half, and then cut the halves into 2-inch pieces. Toss all the pieces in a large bowl with the melted butter and stir to coat. Arrange the bread on a baking sheet and bake for 5 to 8 minutes, until lightly toasted. Set the toasts aside and turn the oven up to 425°F.

- In that same saucepan, melt the remaining 3 tablespoons butter over low heat. Whisk in the flour and continue to whisk until well socialized, but don't let it burn. Slowly add the milk, whisking until a thick paste forms. This is called a *roux*, BTW. It's one of the mother sauces and the key to life, especially when dealing with cheese and meltdowns.

- Now, remove your roux from the heat and fold in the shredded Gruyère and the pancetta and stir until the cheese melts. Season with the nutmeg, salt, and pepper. Spoon the cheese mix over the toasted bread. Return to the oven and bake for another 5 minutes, until the cheese is gooey and golden.

She Asked Me How to Spell *Orange* Chicken

Who are these idiots that can't spell orange?

You might think your gay BFF has dropped you because he wants his pink shirt back, but that's not the case. He wants some of this dish. Hoard it for yourself, unless he's shown up with an autograph from Danny DeVito for you!

SERVES 5

WHAT YA NEED

FOR THE CHICKEN

- 2 pounds boneless skinless chicken breasts
- 2 large eggs
- ½ cup cornstarch
- ¼ cup all-purpose flour
- 1 teaspoon pink salt
- Canola oil

FOR THE SPICY ORANGE SAUCE

- ½ cup freshly squeezed orange juice (or the regular stuff if you're stuck)
- 2 tablespoons low-sodium soy sauce
- 1½ tablespoons rice vinegar
- 2 cloves garlic, pressed through garlic press
- ½ teaspoon grated fresh ginger
- ½ teaspoon red pepper flakes
- 3 tablespoons brown sugar
- 1 tablespoon cornstarch
- 1 tablespoon water

TO SERVE

- Cooked white rice
- Chopped scallions for garnish

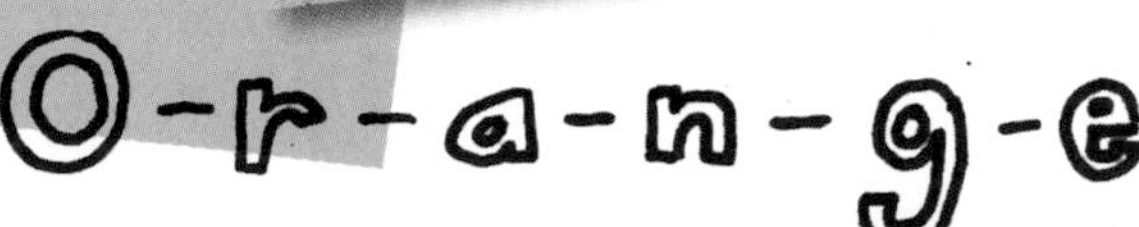

MAKE IT

- Cut your chicken into 1-inch pieces so that they are nice and bite-sized. Set up a dredging assembly line: Crack the eggs into a small bowl and whisk. Mix your cornstarch, flour, and salt together in a separate shallow dish. Then coat each chicken bite in the egg, dredge in the flour mix, and set aside.

- In a large skillet, heat about ¼ inch of canola oil over high heat so it's piping hot and ready to fry. When your oil is ready, add the chicken bites in batches and fry, turning once or twice, 'til golden and cooked through, about 5 minutes. Go slow, and don't crowd the skillet. Transfer the golden bites to a paper towel–lined plate to drain.

- In a saucepan, mix together the orange juice, soy sauce, vinegar, garlic, ginger, red pepper, and brown sugar. Simmer over low heat for approximately 5 minutes, until sugar has dissolved. In a separate bowl, whisk the cornstarch and water to make a slurry. Now, slowly whisk your slurry into your simmering sauce. It will begin to thicken and look like a syrup. At that point, remove from heat. Add the cooked chicken and toss with the sauce. Spoon the chicken and sauce over the cooked white rice, garnish with scallions, and enjoy!

October 3-Bean White Chili

You should probably insure your stomach for $10,000.00.

On October 3rd he asked me to make him the most delicious chili that would break a sweat, put hair on his chest, and make his fork stand up in the bowl. This is a great dish to make on the day you wait for all year . . . #MeanGirlsDay! So grab your fork (or spoon) and start celebrating!

SERVES 6

WHAT YA NEED

FOR THE CHILI

1 (15-ounce) can Great Northern beans, drained

4 cups chicken broth

Olive oil

1 medium sweet onion, diced

3 cloves garlic, minced

1 jalapeño, seeded and diced

½ (12-ounce) can pickled jalapeños, drained

2 (12-ounce) cans diced green chiles

1 (15-ounce) can cannellini beans, drained

1 (15-ounce) can navy beans, drained

3 tablespoons lime juice

2 tablespoons ground cumin

Pink salt and freshly ground black pepper to taste

2½ cups shredded cooked chicken (about 3 small chicken breasts)

Hot sauce to taste

SPECIAL EQUIPMENT
Food processor

MAKE IT

- Combine the Great Northern beans and ½ cup of the chicken broth in a food processor and blend into a thick creamy paste. Set aside.

- Heat a splash of olive oil in a Dutch oven or large stockpot over low heat. Add the onion, garlic, fresh jalapeños, pickled jalapeños, and green chiles and cook for about 10 minutes to let those flavors socialize. Add the pureed beans, remaining 3½ cups chicken broth, the cannellini beans, navy beans, lime juice, cumin, and salt. Stir in the chicken and simmer for a really long time over the lowest heat setting. Let that chili gather some heat and flavor, about 30 minutes Taste as you go and add salt and pepper and hot sauce to your liking, you spicy thang, you ☺.

OPTIONAL GARNISHES

Lime wedges

Fresh cilantro

Shredded Monterey Jack cheese

Chopped avocado

Minced jalapeños (fresh or pickled)

Sour cream or Greek yogurt

- Ladle into bowls and garnish with your favorite toppings. For major bonus points, make a batch of Cornbread Muffins (page 42) to serve on the side.

Why Are You So Obsessed with MEatloaf?

We can't help it if this dish is so popular!

Why didn't you call me back, beyotch? A meat party in your mouth is no excuse. This is NOT your grandma's meatloaf, BTW. This is a Bloody Mary meatloaf. This hearty dish is the ultimate comfort food that will not only cure your hangover but also power your brain up enough to cram for that history final.

SERVES 6

WHAT YA NEED

- Nonstick cooking spray
- ½ cup chopped yellow onion
- 1 tablespoon olive oil
- 1 teaspoon pink salt
- ½ teaspoon black pepper
- ½ teaspoon thyme
- ¼ teaspoon garlic powder
- 2 tablespoons Worcestershire sauce
- ¼ cup Bloody Mary mix
- 2 tablespoons vodka
- 1 teaspoon tomato paste
- 1½ pounds ground turkey (dark and white meat)
- ¾ cup breadcrumbs
- 1 egg, beaten

FOR THE SAUCE

- ¼ cup ketchup
- Pinch brown sugar
- 2 tablespoons Bloody Mary mix

SPECIAL EQUIPMENT

Standard nonstick loaf pan

MAKE IT

- Preheat oven to 350°F and get your aprons on! Grease your standard loaf pan with nonstick cooking spray.

- In a medium sauté pan over medium to low heat, sauté onions, olive oil, salt, pepper, thyme, and garlic powder until soft and slightly golden, approximately 15 minutes. Next add Worcestershire sauce, Bloody Mary mix, vodka, and tomato paste, stirring well so the flavors are well mixed. Let simmer for about 15 minutes and then allow to cool to room temperature.

- Combine the turkey, the breadcrumbs, the egg, and the onion mixture in a large bowl. This should be a fairly wet mixture—that's why the meatloaf comes out so moist—so don't add so many breadcrumbs that you dry it out. Nobody likes dry meat. Nobody. Pour the prepared mixture into your greased loaf pan and cook for 40 to 50 minutes, or until browned. During the last ten minutes of cooking, mix the sauce ingredients in a small bowl and then brush or spoon on top of the loaf. Finish in the oven for an additional 5 to 7 minutes and serve.

Extra credit: CRAM your meat between two buns and you have an awesome Saturday night, errr I mean, SANDWICH! Holla!!!

It's Like, All in Swedish Meatballs

What is the 411 on these meatballs?

So, you've never had Swedish meatballs before? Shut up! *Shut up!*

SERVES 8

WHAT YA NEED

FOR THE MEATBALLS

- Nonstick cooking spray
- ⅓ cup plain breadcrumbs
- ½ cup milk
- 2 tablespoons heavy cream
- 1 large egg
- 1 tablespoon minced fresh parsley
- ½ teaspoon nutmeg
- ¼ teaspoon allspice
- ½ teaspoon kosher salt
- ¼ teaspoon freshly ground black pepper
- 1 tablespoon unsalted butter
- 2 tablespoons olive oil
- ½ medium yellow onion, minced
- 1 large clove garlic, minced
- 1½ pounds ground beef
- 1 pound ground pork

TO SERVE

- Egg noodles or mashed potatoes (optional)
- Lingonberry jam or cranberry sauce (optional)

* OH YEAH *

FOR THE SAUCE

- 7 tablespoons unsalted butter
- ⅓ cup all-purpose flour
- 1 (14½-ounce) can low-sodium beef broth
- 1 (14½-ounce) can low-sodium chicken broth
- 1 cup heavy cream
- ¾ cup sour cream
- 2 tablespoons reduced-sodium soy sauce
- 2 teaspoons Worcestershire sauce
- 2 teaspoons apple cider vinegar
- 1 teaspoon Dijon mustard
- 1 tablespoon sugar
- 1 teaspoon pink salt
- 1 teaspoon freshly ground black pepper
- 2 tablespoons minced fresh parsley

Mini Swedish Lesson

Hello – Hallå

Plastics – Plast

Fetch – Hämta

OMG – Herregud

Bitch – Tik

Balls – Bollar

Thank You – Tack!

MAKE IT

- Preheat your oven to 400°F. Line a couple of baking sheets with foil and lightly coat with nonstick spray.

- In a large bowl, combine the breadcrumbs, milk, cream, egg, parsley, nutmeg, allspice, salt, and pepper. Set aside for a few minutes to let the breadcrumbs soak up the liquids.

- Meanwhile, heat the butter and olive oil in a medium nonstick skillet over medium heat. Add the onion and garlic and sauté for 3 to 5 minutes, until translucent. Add to the breadcrumbs, along with the beef and pork, and incorporate well.

- Roll the meatball mixture into 1- to 2-inch balls and place about 1 inch apart on the prepped baking sheets. Bake for 20 to 25 minutes, until golden brown.

- While the meatballs are cooking, this is the perfect time to make the sauce, check your lipstick, and take a selfie of yourself in the kitchen! Start by melting the butter in a large skillet over low heat, then slowly whisk in the flour. Continue to simmer the butter-flour mix until it turns a little darker . . . you will want a nice light beige color and semi-thick consistency in the end. So keep that in mind. Add the beef and chicken broths, the cream, sour cream, soy sauce, Worcestershire, vinegar, Dijon, sugar, and salt and pepper. Simmer for about 10 minutes, stirring often, until the sauce has thickened. Add the chopped parsley and set aside.

- When the meatballs are golden and piping hot, serve 'em straight up, or over egg noodles or mashed potatoes. Load them up with the sauce and enjoy. If you like, serve with a little sweet and tangy jam, like lingonberry, or cranberry sauce.

POP QUIZ:

~~TRUE~~ DUH OR ~~FALSE~~? SHUT UP

So, you think you have what it takes to be the Queen Bee? Let's see how much you really know with this True or False quiz or, as we like to call it: Duh or Shut Up!

SHUT UP

DUH

SHUT UP

SHUT UP

SHUT UP

DUH

DUH

ANSWER KEY: 1. Duh; 2. Shut up–it's Anfernee; 3. Duh; 4. Shut up–Gretchen's is; 5. Shut up–only two Fendis; 6. Shut up–it's slang from England or . . . something; 7. Duh; 8. Shut up–only half true; 9. Shut up–he's her first cousin, and that is soooo not right; 10. Duh; 11. Duh; 12. Shut up–Taylor only gets two, but Glenn Coco gets four, YOU GO GLENN COCO!; 13. Duh; 14. Shut up–she got gold hoops, but for Hanukkah; 15. Duh; 16. Shut up–she can try Sears.

	DUH	SHUT UP
1. The Plastics only wear jeans or track pants on Fridays.	☐	☐
2. Principal Duvall has a nephew named Anthony.	☐	☐
3. Cady asks Damian and Janis where room G14 is located.	☐	☐
4. Regina's hair is so big because it's full of secrets.	☐	☐
5. Regina has three Fendi purses and a silver Lexus.	☐	☐
6. *Fetch* is slang from Africa.	☐	☐
7. Regina and Aaron went out for a year.	☐	☐
8. Dawn Schweitzer is a fat virgin.	☐	☐
9. It's okay for Karen to make out with Seth Mosakowski, because he's her second cousin.	☐	☐
10. Aaron Samuels is gorgeous.	☐	☐
11. Aaron's hair looks sexy pushed back.	☐	☐
12. Taylor Zimmerman gets three Candy Cane Grams while Glenn Coco gets four!	☐	☐
13. In the "Jingle Bell Rock" performance, Gretchen is always on Regina's left.	☐	☐
14. For Christmas, Gretchen's parents got her this really expensive pair of gold hoop earrings.	☐	☐
15. Nominees for Spring Fling Queen are Regina, Gretchen, Janis, and Cady.	☐	☐
16. When Regina's dress she put on hold doesn't fit, the saleswoman suggests she try Target.	☐	☐

How did you do? If you got more than fourteen right, then you are the Queen Bee. Now just don't go and get hit by a bus, beyotch!

NEW YORK SELTZER

-CHAPTER 6-

Mean Grills (She Doesn't Even Grill Here)

Are you ready to ~~make~~ make out with America's favorite grilled meats? Let's make Amber D'Alessio proud. This chapter includes recipes for your grill that are not only chock-full of flavor, but also won't cause you to singe off your eyebrows. (The au naturale bushy Caroline Krafft look is so in right now, so don't stand too close.) Our Hot as Africa Pepper Chicken (page 112) is so hot it caused the back building to burn down in 1987. We've also got a great burger recipe, so you can take the night off of going to Taco Bell and skip that bathroom line at Barnes & Noble (sorry Gretchen, I know it was an emergency). We even have a great vegetarian option for all those non meat eaters out there. (You know who you are, and so do we because you won't stop telling us.) This bowl of jungle vegetables is sure to make you go *wild,* Principal Duvall style.

Invite your nearest and dearest, put on your ugliest effing skirt, and invite all your Plastic friends over for a balling BBQ. Just remember to ask Ms. Norbury to stop by after she bartends down at T.J. Calamity's; maybe she'll bring you ~~some meth~~

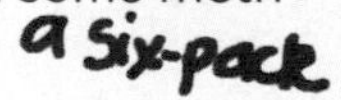

Amber D'Alessio Grilled Hot Dogs

Even if you are only half a virgin, you will still go gaga over these grilled dogs.

Amber may have only done this one time, but you'll be clocking in for these hot dogs daily. Since no one likes a little weenie, make sure you invest in the jumbo dogs. Don't forget to butter the buns. Just let us know if you'd like us to assign someone to butter it for you.

SERVES 1

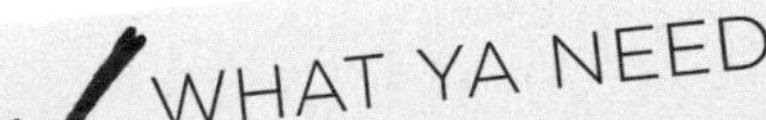

WHAT YA NEED

- 1 long and juicy hot dog
- 1 Hawaiian sweet hot dog bun
- Butter
- Condom-ments

FETCH FACTS

Watch the lip gloss! To this day, Jonathan still claims Rachel McAdams has the softest lips he's ever kissed. Sorry Lindsay!

MAKE IT

Fire up your grill to high and pucker those lips baby! We're about to make the juiciest 6-inch thing you've ever wrapped your mouth around! Well, actually, I can't 100 percent confirm that. But most likely.

- Once your grill is nice and hot, place your dog right on it and cook until you have your desired level of char. Now, toast your buns: Butter that bread and throw it on the grill as well.

- Is it getting hot in here? Go ahead and slip that hot and juicy weiner right into the bun and enjoy. Dress it up with some condom-ments. Mrs. George keeps her house fully stocked. Straight up yellow mustard is my pick.

Best. Rack. Ever.

HA! HA!

A better rack than your old Barbie doll had.

Is your hairline weird? Your pores as big as a house? Are your nailbeds keeping you single? At least you can have the rack of your dreams. These succulent ribs are going to be so epic, your mom will ask who your surgeon, I mean butcher, is.

SERVES 4

WHAT YA NEED

- 2 tablespoons dark brown sugar
- 1 teaspoon paprika
- ½ teaspoon freshly ground black pepper
- ½ teaspoon cumin
- ¾ teaspoon chili powder
- 2 teaspoons ground coffee
- 1¼ teaspoons pink salt
- 2 full racks (about 2 pounds) baby back ribs

- All men really want is a huge juicy rack that they can sink their teeth into. So, get off your treadmill and turn on your grill. We all know a real way to a man's heart is through his stomach. No, seriously, we learned that watching *Grey's Anatomy*—the organs are like kinda connected, but only in men. Don't be fooled: This recipe may be super-simple but is action-packed with flavor.

- Combine the first seven ingredients in a small bowl. Rub the spice mix all over your ribs, lock 'em up in a ziplock bag, and stick it in the fridge overnight so those flavors can socialize.

- When ready to grill, get your apron on. Grilling can be messy. Ribs are really messy. And aprons are super-sexy. Fire up that grill for a robust medium heat. Remove the ribs from the fridge and wrap each rack in heavy-duty aluminum foil; this what I call a flavor packet. It keeps everything moist.

- Grill your meat with the lid down for 20 to 25 minutes. Flip your flavor packets over and cook for another 10 to 15 minutes, until the ribs are fork tender. Remove the ribs from the flavor packets and place directly on the grill over direct heat and crisp them up for 3 to 5 more minutes.

- Remove from the grill and place on a cool wooden board to slice . . . for the 'Gram obvi.

- #BestRackEver #MeanGrills #MyRackBringsTheBoysToTheYard

- By now the smoke and clouds of meat heaven should be hovering over your yard. I imagine there's a line of studs at your front door, just waiting to get in. You're welcome.

Everyone Grab Some RubBURGERS

Even Coach Carr and Trang Pak need to be safe with their meat!

Fighting over a man is so 2004. I mean, that's just like the rules of feminism. Instead try talking about more important sh*t while devouring these amazing BBQ sliders. Like actual human being conversation.

SERVES 4 (MAKES EIGHT 2-OUNCE SLIDERS)

WHAT YA NEED

FOR THE BURGERS

- 1 pound organic ground beef, at least 15 percent fat (remember, fat = flavor)
- 1 tablespoon minced shallot
- 1 clove garlic, minced
- 1 tablespoon whole-grain mustard
- 1 tablespoon ketchup
- 1 teaspoon Worcestershire sauce
- 1 teaspoon sea salt
- 1 teaspoon freshly ground black pepper
- Sliced American cheese
- Slider buns

BURGER TOPPING OPTIONS

- Sliced sweet onion
- Sliced tomato
- Iceberg lettuce
- Sliced bread & butter pickles
- Condom-ments of your liking

Yasss!
Fetch!
DUH
TRUSTEX
Assorted Colors Lubricated Condom

MAKE IT

Whether you grab a *rubber* or a *burger* in this moment could very well be life changing. So choose wisely.

- Start by preheating your grill, you're going to want two heat zones: hot and super-F-ing hot. *Comprende?* Next, in a large bowl, mix the ground beef, shallot, garlic, mustard, ketchup, Worcestershire sauce, salt, and pepper. Get in there with your *bare* hands and make sure the ground beef is well incorporated with the seasonings . . . "no glove no love" does *not* apply here, so just go for it! Mix well, but don't play with the meat too much or it will just get mushy. Grab a palm-size handful and mold an approximately 1½ inch patty. Continue this process 'til you have about 8 patties.

- While the grill is still getting hot, prep your toppings so they are ready when the burgers come hot off the grill. Place the patties on the direct heat or "super hot zone" and cook for about 3 minutes. Flip and cook for an additional 2 minutes on the other side. Lastly, move patties to indirect heat zone, top with the cheese, and close grill lid and let the cheese melt, about 2 minutes.

- Toasting your buns is always a good idea, and you can do this by opening them up and throwing them, cut sides down, on the indirect heat zone for 1 to 2 minutes. Hook up your burger as you wish and dig in!

FETCH FACTS

Plastics and jocks can't be friends, can they? Lindsay Lohan became, like, such good friends with Kaylen Christensen, who is the younger sister of Hayden Christensen, also known as Anakin Skywalker in the *Star Wars* franchise. She plays one of the female jocks and can be seen wearing a blue shirt and a high ponytail during Ms. Norbury's lecture to all of the girls in the gymnasium.

Hot as Africa Pepper Chicken

God Karen, you can't just ask white meat why it's white.

You are probably wondering what makes this chicken African, right? It's not, but keep that secret in your hair, okay. In any case, these smokin' hot breasts look better than the two holes Regina cut out of her shirt to show hers!

SERVES 4

WHAT YA NEED

FOR THE CHICKEN

- 4 boneless skinless chicken breasts
- ¼ cup olive oil
- 1 tablespoon garlic powder
- 2 teaspoons paprika
- Pink salt and freshly ground black pepper to taste

FOR THE AFRICA PEPPER SAUCE

- 10 habanero peppers
- 2 plum tomatoes, coarsely chopped
- 1 medium onion, coarsely chopped
- 4 cloves garlic, peeled and smashed
- 2 fresh basil leaves
- 2 tablespoons fresh parsley leaves
- ¾ cup olive oil
- Pink salt and freshly ground black pepper to taste

MAKE IT

Do you have any friends from Africa? I mean besides Cady, of course. No? Then let me tell you, this sauce is a big deal in Africa. I swear. Like every household, every street meat vendor, and restaurant has a jar of this on hand at all times, because grilled meats are the mainstay food staple. Don't believe me? I've got a book you can read about it. It's in Swedish.

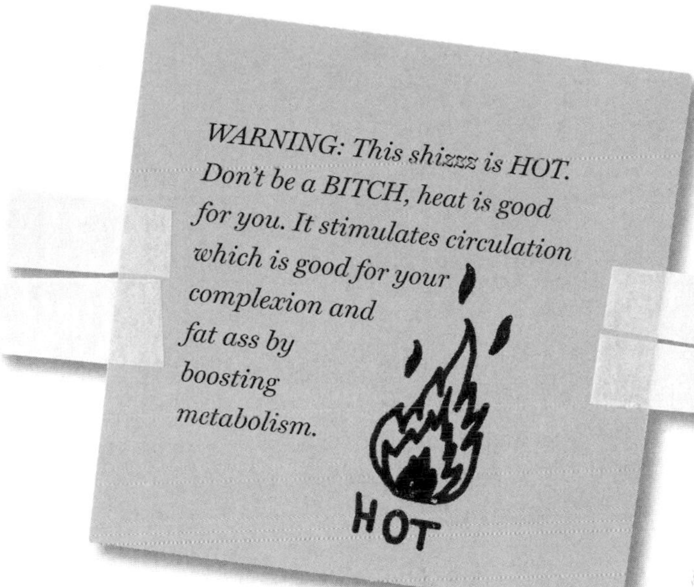

WARNING: This shizzz is HOT. Don't be a BITCH, heat is good for you. It stimulates circulation which is good for your complexion and fat ass by boosting metabolism.
HOT

- Start by firing up that grill to about medium. Then, get your breasts out and grill on! I mean *chicken* breasts, you whore! Place the breasts in a large ziplock bag or plastic wrap and pound with mallet or heavy pan until they are even and slightly flattened. Mix the olive oil, garlic powder, paprika, and salt and pepper in a small bowl, then use to season the breasts on both sides. Grill these beauties over medium heat for about 6 minutes each side, until the meat reaches an internal temp of 165°F.

- Get on that sauce: Remove the stems and seeds from the habanero peppers.

NOTE: Please use gloves when prepping hot peppers! ***DO NOT*** *touch your eyes, face, or anything below your Gucci belt after pepper handling, or your frank & beans/va-jay-jay will burn worse than last semester's STD.*

- Put the habaneros, tomatoes, onion, garlic, basil, parsley, olive oil, and salt and pepper in the food processor and blend until smooth. Pour the sauce into a small saucepan and let simmer over medium heat for about 15 minutes. Slather that sauce on your grilled chicken. Store any extra sauce in a cute Mason jar in the fridge for up to 5 days.

Enjoy, you Skanky Spice Girls!

Homeschooled Jungle Veggie Bowl

Do they eat meat in Girl World?

Well, actually they don't eat anything, but let's not go there. Plus, this recipe needed to be here. Veggie girls are basically gap-toothed Martians to us, but we had to provide at least one non-meat option. Otherwise how would all the vegetarians be able to 'Gram about being vegetarians?

SERVES 2

WHAT YA NEED

- 1 cup farro
- 3 cups vegetable broth
- 1 red bell pepper, seeded and quartered
- 1 medium zucchini, sliced
- 1 medium yellow squash, sliced
- 1 portobello mushroom
- ½ red onion, thickly sliced
- Olive oil for drizzling
- Pink salt and freshly ground black pepper to taste
- 1 cup spinach
- ½ cup Greek yogurt
- Your choice of chopped fresh herbs: mint, parsley, cilantro

FETCH FACTS

The original title for *Mean Girls* was *Homeschooled.*

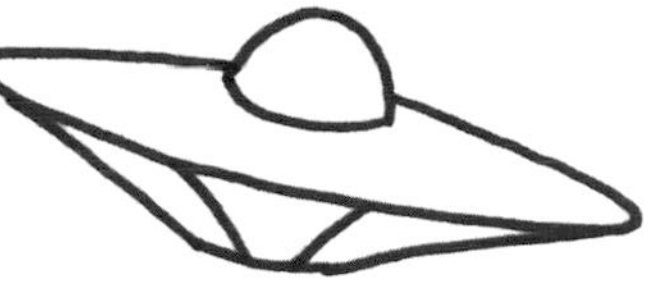

✱ MAKE IT ✱

Okay kids, whether you're homeschooled or not, LUNCH is one of the most important meals of the day. Wherever you sit at North Shore, you need some whole grains and veggies to get past the afternoon hump and not fall over and DIE during 5th period PE.

- So, get your aprons on and start by cooking your farro in the veggie broth according to the package instructions, then set aside.

- While your farro is cooking, FIRE UP THAT GRILL to high to cookie your veg!! You'll want to get a nice char and blisters on these beauties so direct high heat is key. In a small bowl, toss your sliced veggies (pepper, zucchini, squash, mushroom, and onion) with a drizzle of olive oil and some salt and pepper and then throw them on the grill. If you have a veggie grill basket—f*ck yes, go for it! If not, you'll have to just pay careful attention to the grates and try to keep from losing your lunch in the fire hole. Grill those veggies 'til they achieve that gorgeous char we were talking about; 10 minutes should be plenty of time on some fierce fire.

- Gather up the farro, your grilled veggies, and that tasty raw spinach and get ready to assemble your masterpiece. Find your two prettiest bowls and load up! I like to place my ingredients in piles next to each other so they all shine like the superstars they are, and it makes for a super-colorful, highly Insta-worthy dish.

- To dress your bowls, whip together a creamy topping: In another small dish, mix the yogurt with a pinch of salt and dash of olive oil. Use a dollop of this as a cooling creamy sauce, then top the bowls with chopped fresh herbs and dig in!

Health Freak Note: No farro? Substitute brown rice, quinoa, or lentils. Just cook according to package instructions.

SUPER FUN!

NORTH SHORE HIGH SCHOOL CLASS SUPERLATIVES

Next to planning Spring Fling, the most important purpose of the Student Activities Board is to count the votes for class superlatives. You might think you know what you're like, but you could be wrong. Much thought and consideration goes into these and they are all completely accurate!

While you wait for that candy-gram that is never coming, I guess you'll have to give your friends a superlative below! You let it out, honey, put it in the book.

The Gretchen
Most Likely to Join a Cult OR
Biggest Gossip

The Cady
Most Likely to Move Back to Africa and
Never Return to North Shore Again

The Aaron Samuels
Most Likely to Join a Monastery

The Regina
Biggest Drama Queen OR Best Hair

The Damian and Janis
Cutest Couple That Never Was

The Jason
Most Likely to Go to Jail

The Kevin Gnapoor
Most Likely to Be on *Jeopardy!* OR Most Changed

The Karen
Most Likely to Win the Lottery and Lose the Ticket OR Most Likely to Put Whole Fist in Mouth

-CHAPTER 7-

Happy Hour Is from Four to Six

Step aside Mrs. George, this is a job for alcohol, and we've got some drinks that are going to launch happy hour into a whole new hemisphere. Whether it's our Too Gay to Function Cosmo (page 124) or our Why Are You White? Russian (page 120), you will get drunk... and then you will die. Everyone knows that Plastics like to party, and there's no better way to get to know people and make friends than by drinking! It also really brings cousins together and makes whomever you're talking to far less boring. We've also included a non-alcoholic recipe for the underage set—sorry Kylie, maybe next year?

Let's be real though, when we inhale alcohol we exhale happiness, so let the designated drivers, preteens, or those just out of rehab drink the Half a Virgin Piña Colada (page 132) and the rest of you have an awesome time, and Awesome Shooters (page 126) on us.

Why Are You White? Russian

There is a 30 percent chance you will get drunk.

Africa, Russia: same continent? No? Same difference. You still can't ask why it's white. (The cream, duh.) This may feel like a crotchety old cocktail you'd find at T.J. Calamity's, but it's basically an alcoholic chocolate milk fit for a Queen Bee. Trust us. Or you can walk home bitches.

SERVES 1

WHAT YA NEED

Ice
2 ounces vodka (any brand)
2 ounces Kahlúa
3 ounces heavy cream or whole milk
A lot of balls to ask such a question

MAKE IT

This is a one-dump drink. Fill a glass with ice and dump the ingredients in. Stir and drink up.

Regulation Hottie Toddy

This drink is the perfect soup of the day!

Say goodbye to nights of sitting at home alone on those four-way calls wishing some man candy would call through and save you from Gretchen. She's so annoying, just get rid of her already! This drink will make you so popular you will go from a 2 to a 10 in no time. Everyone knows that alcohol makes you lean (against doors and walls, but whatever).

SERVES 1

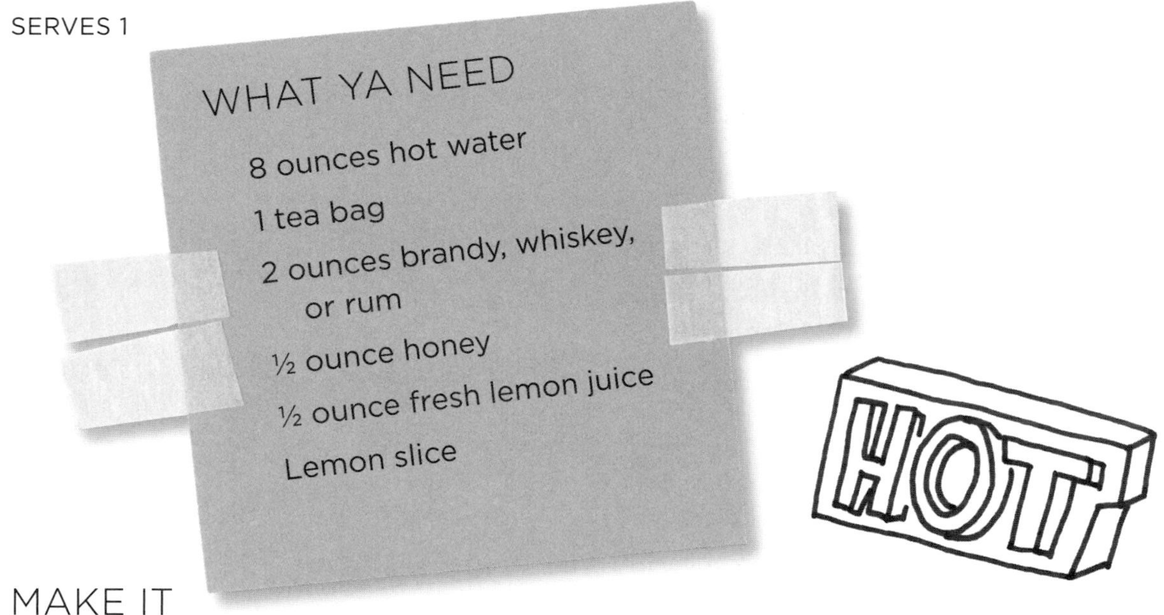

WHAT YA NEED

8 ounces hot water
1 tea bag
2 ounces brandy, whiskey, or rum
½ ounce honey
½ ounce fresh lemon juice
Lemon slice

MAKE IT

You are one hot babe and this tasty nightcap is going to even make you hotter. Since tea is the main thing in the drink, choose wisely: If using as a pre-slumber tincture, I suggest a lovely herbal blend like chamomile. Alternatively, if it's a cold January morning and you're freezing your tits off, then choose a tea that's a bit uplifting, like English Breakfast or a roasted green tea.

- Heat your water in a kettle or in a (microwave-safe) mug in the microwave. Pick your tea, steep in the hot water, and then add the alcohol, honey, and lemon juice. Stir, and enjoy with a slice of fresh lemon and the satisfaction of knowing you're hotter than Regina George.

Test Results on the Rocks

Drink this when you are celebrating good news . . . or bad news.

If you are waiting around for that call from Susan at Planned Parenthood, this drink will make it all better. Well at least for the rest of the day. You know what they say, if your glass is half empty, then fill it up again and again!

SERVES 1

WHAT YA NEED

- 1 bottle Jameson Irish Whiskey
- Ice cubes
- Application to a new school

MAKE IT

It's a sunny and 72-degree kind of Thursday afternoon. Life is good. Homework is done. You're having an awesome hair day . . . then all of a sudden the phone rings. Someone answers before you can pause from painting your toenails to grab it. From the bottom of the stairs you hear screeching, and you know that if the doctor's office is calling, it can't be good news!

- Pour 2 to 10 ounces of Jameson in glass over ice and CHUG.
- Pick a friend from your top five to call (tell one friend only because juicy gossip like this spreads quicker than the STD you probably have).
- Repeat Step 1 and call the last person you plowed so they don't start a pandemic.

Skanky Beyotches Note: Condoms are free at Planned Parenthood health centers. Learn your lesson so you never have to make this recipe again.

Too Gay to Function Cosmo

Step aside Damian, this is a job for alcohol.

This drink will get your nana so drunk she'll take off her wig. And after you down a few of these yourself, every guy in the room will start to look like a hottie to you. Who needs a pink polo shirt when you have this cocktail to accessorize with? Plus, it gives you a nice dose of vitamin C and can stave off any impending UTIs.

SERVES 4

WHAT YA NEED

- 1 (750-milliliter) bottle vodka
- 2 ounces triple sec
- 2½ ounces cranberry juice
- 1½ ounces fresh lime juice
- Lime wedges for garnish
- Plate of granulated sugar for the rim (optional)

FETCH FACTS

The character Damian is based on an old friend of Tina Fey's.

MAKE IT

Open your bottle of vodka and take a shot for good measure. Depending on how many friends you have in tow, or how *white-girl-wasted* you really want to be, I suggest you start with a batch of four cosmos.

- Mix 1 cup vodka with the triple sec, cranberry juice, and lime juice in a super-jumbo cocktail shaker or pitcher. Before filling glasses, use a lime wedge to wet each rim and then dip the rim into the plate of sugar. CONGRATULATIONS! You just gave yourself a sugared rim job. You've out-gayed yourself. Now distribute the drinks amongst garnished glasses and serve!

Impress-Your-Gayest-of-Friends Note: Chill your glasses in the freezer for 10 minutes before serving. This ensures an ice-cold cosmo, and makes your glasses look cute and frosty.

Awesome Shooters

Shooters taste best when you're having an awesome time at your awesome party with awesome music.

Feeling like the art freaks have ganged up on you because you didn't make it to their show? Whatever, throw one (or five) of these awesome shots back and you'll be back in Plastic world in no time! And if you are getting the guilt trip because your artsy friend won first prize and you *still* weren't there to see it . . . then shoot back another. Repeat until you feel awesome again.

SERVES 12

WHAT YA NEED

- 1 (750-milliliter) bottle sparkling pink Moscato (3 cups)
- 4 envelopes (1 ounce) Knox unflavored gelatin
- 3 tablespoons cane sugar
- 1 cup vodka
- 1 drop pink food coloring
- Sanding sugar for garnish

MAKE IT

- Pour 2 cups of the Moscato into a small saucepan and add the gelatin. No heat just yet: Allow the gelatin to bloom for about 2 minutes. Add the sugar and bring to a simmer over low heat, then simmer for a few minutes, until the gelatin and sugar dissolve. Remove from the heat and set aside.

- In a separate bowl, mix the remaining 1 cup Moscato with the vodka and food coloring. Add the hot gelatin mix to the cool vodka mix and stir to combine. Distribute your pink goodness evenly amongst mini plastic cups or cute heart-shaped molds like I did. I even saw small penis-shaped molds at the arts and crafts store . . . whatever you choose will be awesome. Lightly coat the mold with nonstick spray (to ensure an easy escape).

- Allow these beauties to cool and set in the refrigerator for at least 4 hours or, better yet, overnight. For extra awesomeness, and a super 'Gram-worthy masterpiece, sprinkle sanding sugar on top of your shooters! Then go ahead and soak up each other's awesomeness.

FETCH FACTS

In an alternative ending that didn't fly, Kevin G. was supposed to get busted for selling drugs by Ms. Norbury. She then confiscates them and puts them in her desk. After she's accused of being a "pusher" in the burn book, the cops find the drugs in her desk and she's arrested.

High Status Man-hattan Candy

Drink this if you have two Fendi purses and a silver Lexus.

Behind every popular woman is a band of loyal followers and a fine piece of high status man candy. A good woman knows that the way to a man's heart is through his stomach, and often via a pint glass. Whether you are hobnobbing with John Stamos on a plane, or are in for a quiet evening at home with that hottie jock from the soccer team, there is one thing for certain, this drink will be your spirit animal. We should know after all, we like invented it.

SERVES 1

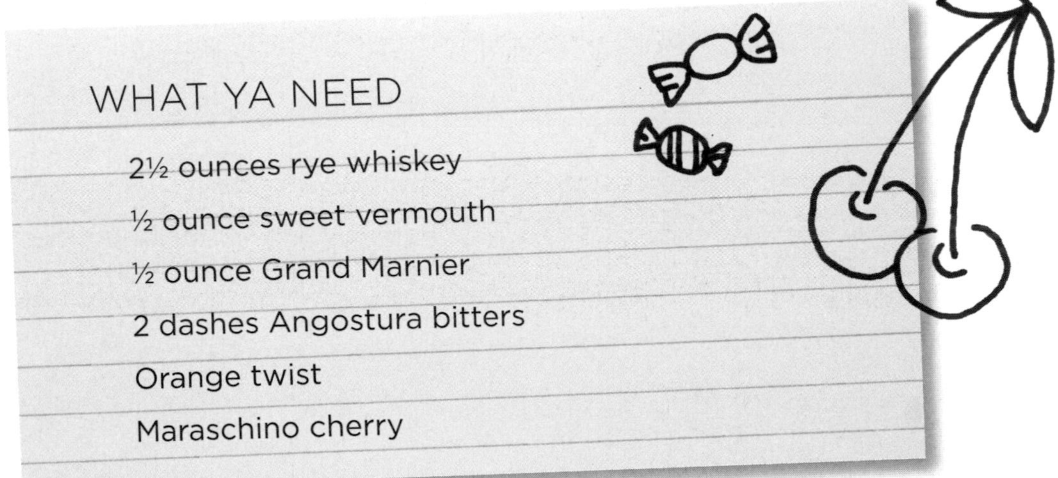

WHAT YA NEED

- 2½ ounces rye whiskey
- ½ ounce sweet vermouth
- ½ ounce Grand Marnier
- 2 dashes Angostura bitters
- Orange twist
- Maraschino cherry

MAKE IT

First things first, dim the lights, throw on some jazz, and head to your bar cart. If you don't have a bar cart, for God's sake, woman, go on Pinterest and start curating one immediately.

- Now, gather up the first four ingredients and STIR—don't shake—in a chilled cocktail shaker. Pour the mix delicately into a short whiskey glass. Serve neat with an orange twist and a cherry.

You Can't Sip with Us

Are you wearing sweatpants on Monday? What about a disgusting vest? Well buckle up, things are about to get mean!

This drink is so perfect that even your parents will trade bedrooms with you, so start sipping. You will even ensure yourself a perma-spot every day at the lunch table, no matter what you're wearing.

SERVES 1

WHAT YA NEED

½ cup ice cubes

½ cup rosé wine, chilled

1 ounce St-Germain (elderflower liqueur)

Cute AF glassware

Heavy splash sparkling water

Lemon or grapefruit slice for garnish

Pink outfit

Sassy 'tude

MAKE IT

- This is another dump-and-run cocktail. (No more diarrhea jokes, Gretchen, we promise!) Grab the ice, rosé, and St-Germain and stir in a chilled cocktail shaker. Pour into your super-cute glass, top off with sparkling water, and garnish away.
- Snap a pic for the 'Gram: #MeanGrills #YouCantSipWithUs #OnWednesdaysWeDrinkPink. *Cheers, babes!*

You Go, Glenn (Hot) Coco

This hot cocoa is flawless!

This drink is richer than Gretchen Wieners's dad. You will want to cash in your four candy-grams for four mugs of this amazing chocolate goodness. Do you want to add whipped cream . . . of course you do, you slut.

SERVES 1

WHAT YA NEED

1 cup milk

2 tablespoons unsweetened cocoa powder

1 to 2 tablespoons sugar (to taste)

Pinch kosher salt

¼ teaspoon vanilla extract (use the real shizz, not imitation)

FETCH FACTS

David Reale, also known as Glenn Coco, got more than four candy canes when he snuck onto set. Director Mark Waters recognized him from passing over him during casting for another part and cast him as Glenn Coco as consolation.

MAKE IT

Maybe you aced your algebra exam, maybe you automatically became head of the Student Activities Committee, or maybe you just woke up feeling like the F-ing rock star you are and wanted to *Treat Yo Self.* Well, you go Glenn *(hot)* Coco, you G-O!!

- Whisk together 2 tablespoons of the milk, the cocoa powder, sugar, and salt in a small saucepan over low heat. Slowly, with some swag, stir in the rest of the milk, whisking gently until it is just hot enough to simmer. Remember, burnt milk sucks so don't get too carried away. Once the milk's bubbling a little bit, not burning, add the vanilla and serve.

Note: Milk can come from any animal you prefer, or nuts, or another botanical source like a coconut. (In case ya didn't know, coconuts are part of the drupe seed family and, botanically speaking, not a nut.) And by nut milk, I mean milk made from almonds, cashews, or macadamias, you filthy whores.

Half a Virgin Piña Colada

For those who don't drink alcohol, but still have a fat ass.

Well here's to sobriety! Three cheers for you. You don't have to be a life-ruiner or a party-ruiner because there's always this delicious option. All of the alcoholics at the party will have a BIG LESBIAN crush on you as they beg for a sip. It's that good! Bonus: Use a straw and you can suck it through your gap-teeth!

SERVES 1

WHAT YA NEED

- ½ banana
- 1 cup fresh pineapple chunks
- 1 cup canned coconut milk (full-fat, babes)
- ¼ cup heavy cream
- ¼ cup sugar
- 1 teaspoon vanilla extract
- 1 cup crushed ice
- Pineapple slice for garnish

MAKE IT

First things first, grab that banana. Peel it, eat half, and save the other half for the drink.

- Add the banana half and the remaining ingredients to your blender and pulse on high until smooth and creamy. Pour into glass of choice and garnish with a fresh pineapple wedge. *Aloha, beyotches!*

Healthy Beyotches Note: Add 2 scoops of whey protein to make this colada a meal replacement bevy, action-packed with good fats, potassium, and vitamin C!

FAT
ASS
VIRGIN

LET'S PARTY!

The Boozy Burn Brunch

Stop trying to be so F-ing popular and dig deep into that fugly slut that's hiding out in everybody. It's time to turn your basic brunch into a *boozy brunch*. But only use alcohol if you're old enough to drink, I mean what kind of person do you think I am? (Why, do you want a little? Because if you do I'd rather you do it in the house.)

To get started, make sure everyone has a full drink ready to go, obviously one of our drinks because they are amazeballs. Watch the movie, and don't cheat. Grool?

THE FOUR TO SIX DRINKING GAME

Take one drink when:

- The movie starts
- "Girl World" is mentioned
- Anyone says "the Plastics"
- Anyone says "Regina George"
- Aaron Samuels appears

Assign one drink when:

- Someone mispronounces Cady's name
- You hear the word *sex*
- Someone tries to make *fetch* happen
- Someone says "Africa"

Take two drinks when:

- Something is crossed off the List to Destroy Regina
- People start acting like animals
- Coach Carr comes on screen
- A four-way call attack happens
- Aaron tries to do math
- Aaron kisses someone

Waterfall when:

- "Jingle Bell Rock" happens (whoever knows the most choreography doesn't have to waterfall)

Finish your drink when:

- Someone gets hit by a bus

#BurnBrunch

HOW TO THROW A #BURNBRUNCH:

STEP 1. Make all the drinks you just read about in chapter 7.

STEP 2. Make all the pretty foods and bevys from chapter 4.

STEP 3. Arrange everything on a table with pretty stuff.

STEP 4. Invite your favorite beeyotches or Plastics.

STEP 5. Put on your most favorite pink outfit.

STEP 6. Take pics and hashtag your masterpiece #BurnBrunch.

STEP 7. Cheers!!!

-CHAPTER 8-

Get In, Loser, It's Desserts

Whether you go here or not, dessert is always the answer to whatever the question may be. Now, in the past your Plastic friends have passed on dessert because how will they fit into their 1-3-5? But once they get a load of these masterpieces, every day will be a sweatpants-from-Sears day!

There is going to be so much sweet bliss in the room that everyone will get along, just like they used to in middle school. We have even provided a cake of rainbows and smiles that is perfect for any occasion. Janis Ian will be excited over our peppermint bark that smells as good as her foot cream, but should not be smeared over any body part . . . well unless you're in private. Don't forget to save room for our special recipe for Hump Day Peanut Butter Balls (page 146). You will probably want to eat them yourselves and not give any out, well at least not to Gretchen Wieners. Bye.

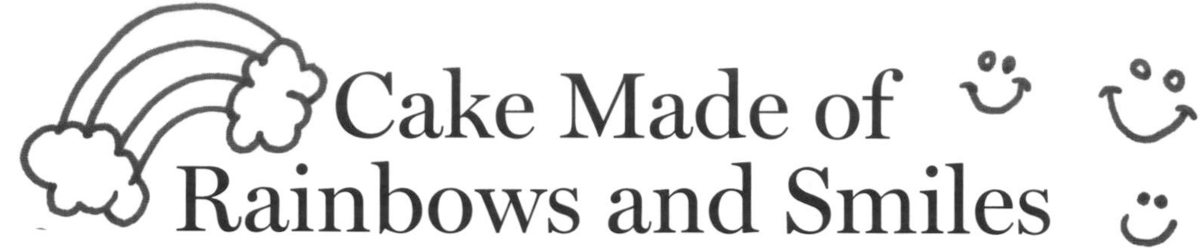

Cake Made of Rainbows and Smiles

Just eat it and be happy.

This cake will leave you wanting to fall into a mosh pit of girls. Not only is it covered in pink and simply gorgeous, it's filled with all kinds of artificial ingredients so it's fake AF (just like that apology, *Gretchen*). In fact, the key to making this cake taste just like the kind you had at your fairy princess seventh birthday party is that you absolutely must use that fake, cheap vanilla extract and those brightly colored artificial sprinkles from the Dollar Store. #Sorrynotsorry. That's what makes it Plastic. And delicious.

SERVES 10

WHAT YA NEED

FOR THE CAKE

- Nonstick cooking spray
- 1 cup (2 sticks) unsalted butter, at room temperature
- 1½ cups sugar
- Whites of 3 large eggs, separated
- 1 large egg (white and yolk)
- 2¼ tablespoons vanilla extract (the clear imitation stuff works here!)
- 5 tablespoons vegetable oil
- 2½ cups cake flour
- 2¼ teaspoons baking powder
- ¾ teaspoon salt
- 1 cup whole milk
- 1 cup sprinkles

FOR THE FROSTING

- 2 cups (4 sticks) unsalted butter, at room temperature
- 3½ cups powdered sugar, or to taste
- 3 teaspoons vanilla extract (the clear imitation stuff works here!)
- 1 pinch salt
- Pink food coloring

SPECIAL EQUIPMENT

Standing mixer, 2 (8-inch) cake pans, cake stand

MAKE IT

Grab your standing mixer and aprons, babes. We are making a cake from SCRATCH!

- Preheat oven to 350°F. Spray your 8-inch cake pans with nonstick spray.
- In your standing mixer, beat the butter and sugar until it's nice and fluffy. Add in the egg whites one at a time, then crack the last egg and add it whole. Mix in the imitation vanilla and vegetable oil.
- In a separate medium-size bowl, whisk flour, baking powder, and salt until combined. Slowly add this dry mix into your wet ingredients in small batches, while running your mixer at low speed. Take your time with this step—each batch of dry should be incorporated fully before you dump the next. Then slowly incorporate the milk. Once everything is mixed and smoothed out, toss in your sprinkles and mix those in by hand.

- Divide the batter evenly between the cake pans and bake until a toothpick comes out clean if you stick it in the center. Start checking at around 23 to 25 minutes so you don't overbake it. Once done, let cakes cool in their pans on a wire rack.

- While the cakes are cooling, make your frosting. Beat all of the frosting ingredients (except food coloring) in a standing mixer. While mixing, add in a couple of drops of food coloring at a time to determine which shade of Plastic Pink will best suit your cake. Taste as you go, adding more sugar if needed to keep a spreadable frosting consistency. Once frosting is smooth and pink, set aside.

- Carefully remove cooled cakes from their pans. Using a long, serrated knife, cut each in half lengthwise, so you have 4 cake rounds to stack up and layer in your final cake!

- Add a layer of frosting to the top of 3 rounds and stack them up on your prettiest of cake stands. Add the final round to the top of the pile and evenly frost the outside of all the layers. Decorate as you please! Maybe more sprinkles, maybe a candied unicorn, a tiara, maybe you're a purist and just want frosting . . . this is your Plastic World, honey—in this world you *can* have your cake and eat it too! Snap a pic of your creation before you plant your face in it. #CakeFullOfRainbowsAndSmiles

Hack That Cake!

The Fun-Fetchy Cake

If the Plastics had a mascot, this cake would be it!

Okay babes, you want a cake of rainbows and smiles but short on time and cash? This cake mix hack is everything. We F-ing *love* Funfetti—everybody loves Funfetti—and if there's a quicker way to get to the same results, we'll take it. More time for champagne drinking and pillow fights, amiright? We've kicked up the ingredients a notch from what the box calls for and, we promise, it will taste like it just came hot off the set of *Cake Wars.* JB has seen a sh*t ton of cakes in his life and THIS ONE is by far his fav. Eat it alone, share it with friends, whatever . . . just don't give any to that scum-sucking road whore who ruined your life.

SERVES 10

WHAT YA NEED

FOR THE CAKE

- Nonstick cooking spray
- 1 (15¼-ounce) box Funfetti Premium Cake Mix
- 4 large eggs
- ⅔ cup (1⅓ sticks) butter, melted
- 1 cup milk
- Rainbow sprinkles for decorating

FOR THE FROSTING

- 1 cup whipping cream
- 1 (16-ounce) container vanilla frosting
- Pink food coloring

SPECIAL EQUIPMENT

- Electric mixer, 2 (8-inch) cake pans, cake stand

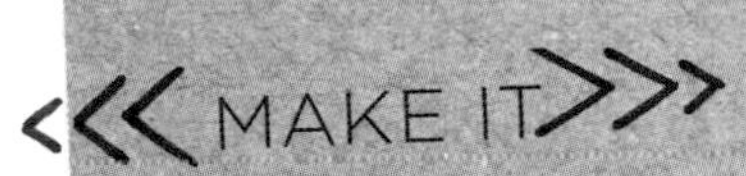

MAKE IT

Get your apron ON and cake stand OUT, you will most def want to put this beauty on display! Oh, and preheat your oven to 350°F. And be sure to grease up those cake pans with nonstick spray.

- In a large metal mixing bowl, dump in the cake mix. Add the eggs, melted butter, and milk. Stir until well mixed. Divide the batter evenly between the 2 prepped cake pans and bake for 13 to 17 minutes, until a toothpick comes out clean if you stick it in the center. Let the cakes cool in their pans on a wire rack. Go have a glass of wine or something, until they are cool to the touch.

- While the cakes cool, make the frosting. In a separate bowl, beat the cream with an electric mixer until peaks form. Then beat in the frosting and a couple drops of food coloring to get that *pink* you want. It should look light and creamy.

- Carefully remove cooled cakes from their pans. Using a long, serrated knife, cut each in half lengthwise, so you have 4 cake rounds to stack up and layer in your final cake! Add a layer of frosting to the top of 3 rounds and stack them up on your prettiest of cake stands. Add the final round to the top of the pile and evenly frost the outside of all the layers. Decorate with sprinkles or whatever your precious heart desires.

Face Smells Like a Foot Peppermint Bark

Even the Marymount Prep boys will be lining up to take a whiff of this one.

If you're grounded but you go out anyways, your parents can't really be mad when they get home from the Ladysmith Black Mambazo concert—if you leave them a plate of this minty chocolate bark. Just don't try to smear it all over your face.

MAKES ABOUT 2 POUNDS

WHAT YA NEED

- 12 ounces semisweet chocolate, chopped into ½-inch pieces
- 1½ teaspoons peppermint extract
- 1 pound white chocolate, chopped into ½-inch pieces
- 3 candy canes, crushed

SPECIAL EQUIPMENT

- 2 heat-safe bowls

FETCH FACTS

After *Mean Girls*, Jonathan and Lacey Chabert worked together in three more movies: *Slightly Single in L.A.*, *Anything Is Possible*, and Hallmark's *Elevator Girl*.

MAKE IT

Get ready, we're about to embark on some baking chocolatiering-technical shizz. Pay attention (KAREN) or your peppermint bark will taste like bark from a tree. The kind that a dog pissed on. Burnt chocolate sucks.

- First things first, get your aprons on, then line a 9x13-inch baking dish with foil, shiny side up. In a small saucepan over medium-high heat, bring 2 inches of water to a gentle boil. Place a heat-safe bowl over the saucepan (now acting as a double boiler). Don't let the bowl touch the water! Lower the heat and add ¾ cup of the semisweet chocolate to the bowl, stirring as it melts. Add another ¾ cup chocolate and keep stirring. Be patient, don't check your Insta or Snap RN, watch the damn chocolate. This will take some time, maybe even a whole 10 minutes. Once all of your chocolate is melted, add ¾ teaspoon of the peppermint extract and let those flavors socialize for just a sec, then swiftly pour the melted chocolate into the lined baking dish to create a nice even layer. Let that sit for 10 minutes.

- Then do basically the same shizz, but with the white chocolate. Use a clean bowl and working with a bit more white chocolate at a time—so begin with 1 cup of white chocolate chunks, melt . . . blah blah blah . . . Add your peppermint extract and then swiftly pour this white layer over the brown layer in your baking dish.

- Last but not least, sprinkle with crushed candy canes and walk away so it can firm up. Once solid, break your bark! Use a knife, small hammer, your little brother's face . . . whatever works.

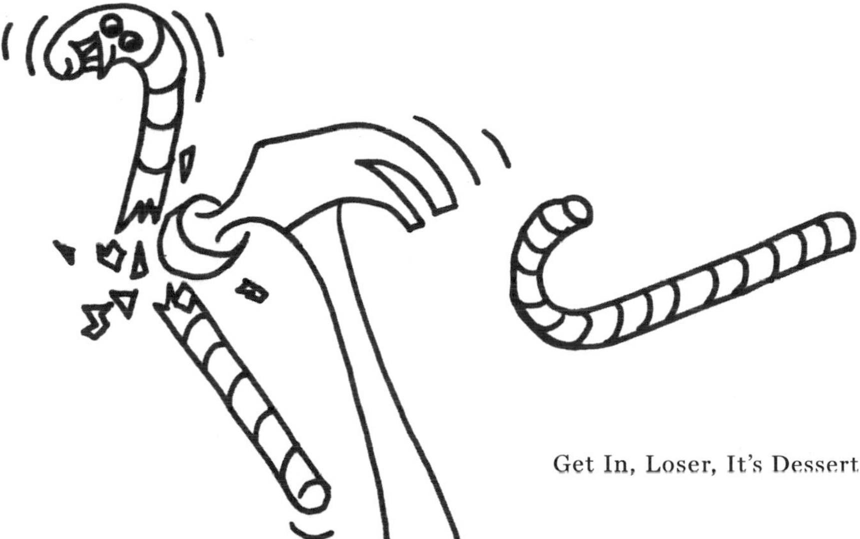

Hump Day Treat: Peanut Butter BALLS

When you have the condoms, but need the snack. God love ya

If Mrs. George offers to get you anything, like some snacks, a condom, or these peanut butter BALLS, put a hold on the make-out sesh and grab some.

MAKES A LOT OF BALLS

WHAT YA NEED

- 1½ cups sifted powdered sugar
- 3 tablespoons butter or margarine, softened
- ½ cup creamy peanut butter
- 1 pound dipping chocolate

SPECIAL EQUIPMENT

- Wax paper

FETCH FACTS

At first Paramount didn't want Tim Meadows and Amy Poehler to star in *Mean Girls* because they were afraid that it would be perceived as a *Saturday Night Live* movie.

De-Lish

MAKE IT

These balls are so easy, it's almost stupid. They also are incredibly tasty and action-packed with protein. I mean, raise your hand if you want a salty and sweet protein load on Hump Day!

Right, I thought so.

- In a medium bowl with a wooden spoon, carefully mix the powdered sugar, the butter, and the peanut butter until it forms a thick dough. Using your clean bare hands, grab some of the dough and shape into a nice uniform, 1-inch round ball. Place on a wax paper–covered baking sheet. Repeat ball sculpting 'til there's no more dough. Let the balls rest for 20 minutes. They need a nap.

- In the meantime, melt your dipping chocolate according to package directions and set aside.

- Once the balls have finished napping, use a fork to gently dip your balls into the chocolate, one ball at a time please, then place back on the wax paper and let those babies dry. I like my balls half dipped, it's kinda like the game "just the tip" but with food. But you can go balls deep if you want 'em all smothered in chocolate all the way around.

- Pop in as many balls that you can fit in your mouth and enjoy! Store the rest in the fridge for up to 5 days.

High Maintenance Beyotches Note: If you or a loved one within 20 feet of you have an anaphylactic allergy to peanuts, DO NOT make this recipe.

Ms. Norberry Pie

This pie is a personal favorite of Randy from Chase Visa.

Did you just get home from bartending at T.J. Calamity's, only to realize your shirt is stuck to your sweater and your bra was probably showing all night? Well then open the fridge and bury your face in this berry pie! If teaching pi to teenagers can't bring you joy, bingeing away your sorrows on pie sure will.

MAKES 1 PIE

YUM

WHAT YA NEED

- 1 refrigerated pie crust (store-bought, unless your name is Martha Stewart, in which case go ahead and make them from scratch)
- 1 refrigerated lattice pie crust for topper
- 7 cups fresh or frozen raspberries, blueberries, and blackberries (about 2⅓ cups each)
- 1 cup sugar (or more), plus a little extra to sprinkle on top of the pie
- 1 tablespoon lemon juice
- ¼ cup cornstarch
- 2 tablespoons unsalted butter
- 1 egg white, beaten with a fork
- Whipped cream for serving (optional)

MAKE IT

- Turn your oven on to 400°F. Open your pie crusts and fit one in a lightly greased pie pan to create the bottom crust.

- Grab all your berries, sugar, and lemon juice and put in a large saucepan. Simmer over medium heat until warm and juicy, about 7 minutes. Stir a couple times to keep things moving as they cook. Take a taste to see if you want it sweeter. Personally, we like ours a bit more on the tart side, but if you feel the need for sweet (or you're naturally a salty bitch and require more sweetener), go ahead and add an extra ¼ cup sugar now.

- Spoon out ½ cup of the berry juice from the saucepan and put into a small bowl. Add the cornstarch and blend 'til smooth. (This is what you call making a slurry, which is totally different than slurry speech from too much rosé.) Make sure to blend in the little white cornstarch clumps or they will explode like a cocaine ball of magma in the pie, which is not fun.

- Now, go back to your pot of berries and bring 'em back to a nice simmer. Slowly stir in your slurry. Don't smash your berries as you stir. Wait a couple of minutes 'til it all thickens up.

- Remove the saucepan from the heat and stir in the butter. Pour the mixture into the pie shell, top with the second latticed crust. Pinch the edges of the top and bottom pie crusts to give it a nice '80s crimp. Brush the pie with the beaten egg white and sprinkle with sugar.

- Bake for 40 to 45 minutes, until crust is golden. But give it a check after 25 to make sure your sh*t's not on fire, and at that point you will probably want to cover the pie with foil for the remaining cook time.

- Place on a wire rack or somewhere safe so it can cool. Although tempting, don't dig in for a few hours or your whipped cream will melt like butter and slide right off. Dollop individual slices with whipped cream, if you like.

PLASTICS BEAUTY TIP

After brushing egg white on pie crust, feel free to brush some on your washed face and let sit for 20 minutes, or until your face becomes so tight you can't blink. Rinse with warm water. Your face should look like you just had a Botox party and eyelid lift all in one! You're welcome.

Note: Since it has all kinds of berries, which is a fibrous fruit, this pie is basically a smoothie and therefore can be eaten at breakfast. Enjoy, beyotches.

Strawberry Toaster Doodles

Mr. Wieners's greatest invention.

Gretchen Wieners's dad is the master behind this toaster strudel. We thought we'd expose his secret recipe, straight from Gretchen's big hair!

MAKES 8 DOODLES

WHAT YA NEED

- ¾ cup strawberry jam
- 1 tablespoon cornstarch mixed with 1 tablespoon cold water
- 2 sheets frozen puff pastry, thawed
- 1 cup powdered sugar
- 1 to 2 tablespoons fresh lemon juice
- Red food coloring

High Maintenance Beyotches Note: If you happen to be allergic/GF/vegan/paleo/keto/whatever, or just flat out don't like strawberries, then you are free to sub with almost any fruit jam.

MAKE IT

Some losers get store-bought strudels, which just keeps making Gretchen's dad rich AF. But real beyotches make their own breakfast pastry from scratch.

- Set your oven to 425°F. Bring the jam and cornstarch and water mixture to a boil in a small saucepan over low to medium heat. Don't let it burn, burnt jam tastes like ass. Stir for 3 to 4 minutes and then set aside to cool to room temp.

- Lay out one sheet of your puff pastry and cut into 4 rectangles. Scoop a hefty spoonful of the thickened and cooled jam in the middle of one end of each piece. Fold those beauties in half and seal like a love letter with a solid '80s crimp using a fork. Repeat with the next 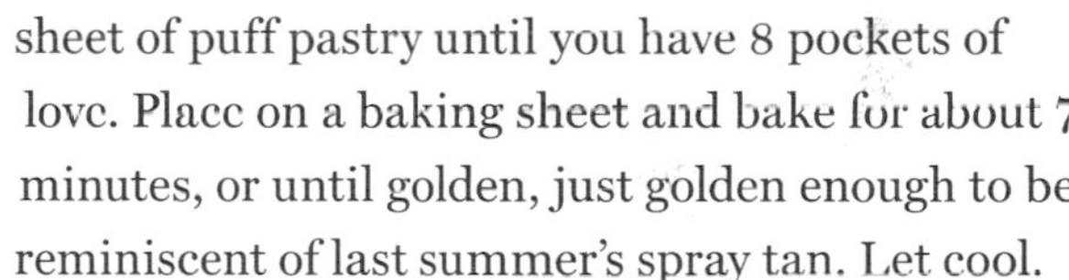 sheet of puff pastry until you have 8 pockets of love. Place on a baking sheet and bake for about 7 minutes, or until golden, just golden enough to be reminiscent of last summer's spray tan. Let cool.

- While baking, whisk the powdered sugar and lemon juice together in a small bowl, adding juice only a ½ tablespoon at a time. This is gonna be icing, so you'll want a glossy and thick consistency. Add a few drops of red food coloring and stir. Once your strudels have cooled, drizzle with icing. Let icing set for about 30 minutes before you dig in!

Note: This is technically a "breakfast food." But there are no rules here. If you're over 21 these beauties go great with champagne!

Crack Rock Candy

Do you wanna buy some drugs?

Are you a pusher? You're definitely gonna wanna push this crack on people. This candy is so good that you will become addicted and then you will die. Just kidding. But eat too much of it and you might just be too fat to outrun that bus . . . and then you'll die.

MAKES 1 KILO

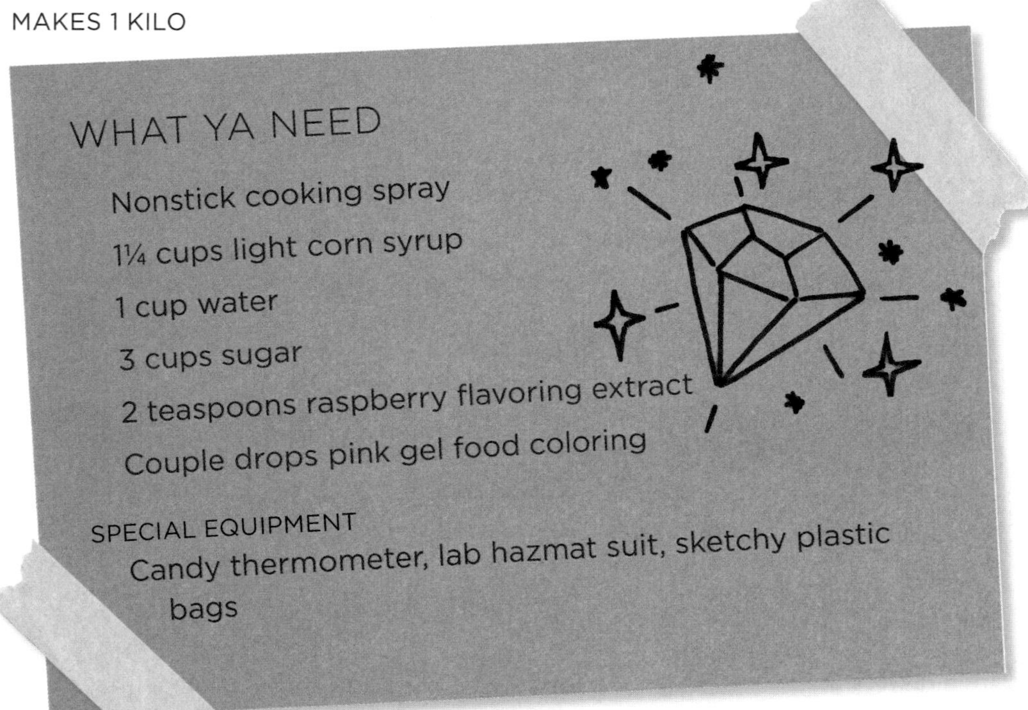

WHAT YA NEED

Nonstick cooking spray

1¼ cups light corn syrup

1 cup water

3 cups sugar

2 teaspoons raspberry flavoring extract

Couple drops pink gel food coloring

SPECIAL EQUIPMENT

Candy thermometer, lab hazmat suit, sketchy plastic bags

MAKE IT

Why BUY drugs when you can DIY that shizz and make your own? Grab your lab coat, beyotches, because we're *Baking Bad* in here today!!

- Step 1 (not to be confused with the 12-step program, that's *after* the crack rock): Line a baking sheet with foil and spray the foil with nonstick cooking spray.

• Next, in large saucepan with a candy thermometer attached, bring the corn syrup, water, and sugar to a boil, stirring as the sugar dissolves. Once dissolved, stop stirring and continue to cook until the thermometer reads 300°F. Remove from heat and let cool, until the mixture stops bubbling. Add the flavoring extract and a couple drops of food coloring and stir to fully incorporate. Next, immediately pour your batch of crack onto the baking sheet and lift it from side to side to distribute the mixture evenly. Be extra careful. The mixture will be molten hot. It doesn't have to be perfect and holes are okay. Let the crack sit and cool at room temperature for a couple hours.

• Once it has hardened into the pure pink rock we're all jonesing for, grab a spoon, hair brush, calculator, anything within reach, and break that rock up into ½- to 1-inch shards.

• Distribute the broken bits evenly amongst your sketchy plastic bags. Word of advice, even though this is CANDY, it is not a good idea to hand this out to kids, especially strange kids in a park.
Just saying.

Disclaimer Note: This is not a recipe for real drugs. We are not endorsing real drugs. Just say NO to real drugs. Especially crack and meth; they will make your extensions fall out and your face age and wrinkle at lightning speed. If you or a loved one are ever tempted, just Google faces of meth. *'Nuff said.*

Milkshake-It Like 2004

This shake will bring all the boys to the yard!

Every math enthusiast will be giving you his card, his varsity jacket, and maybe his virginity after trying this milkshake. This is truly the bomb! Just make sure it's shaken and not stirred.

SERVES 1

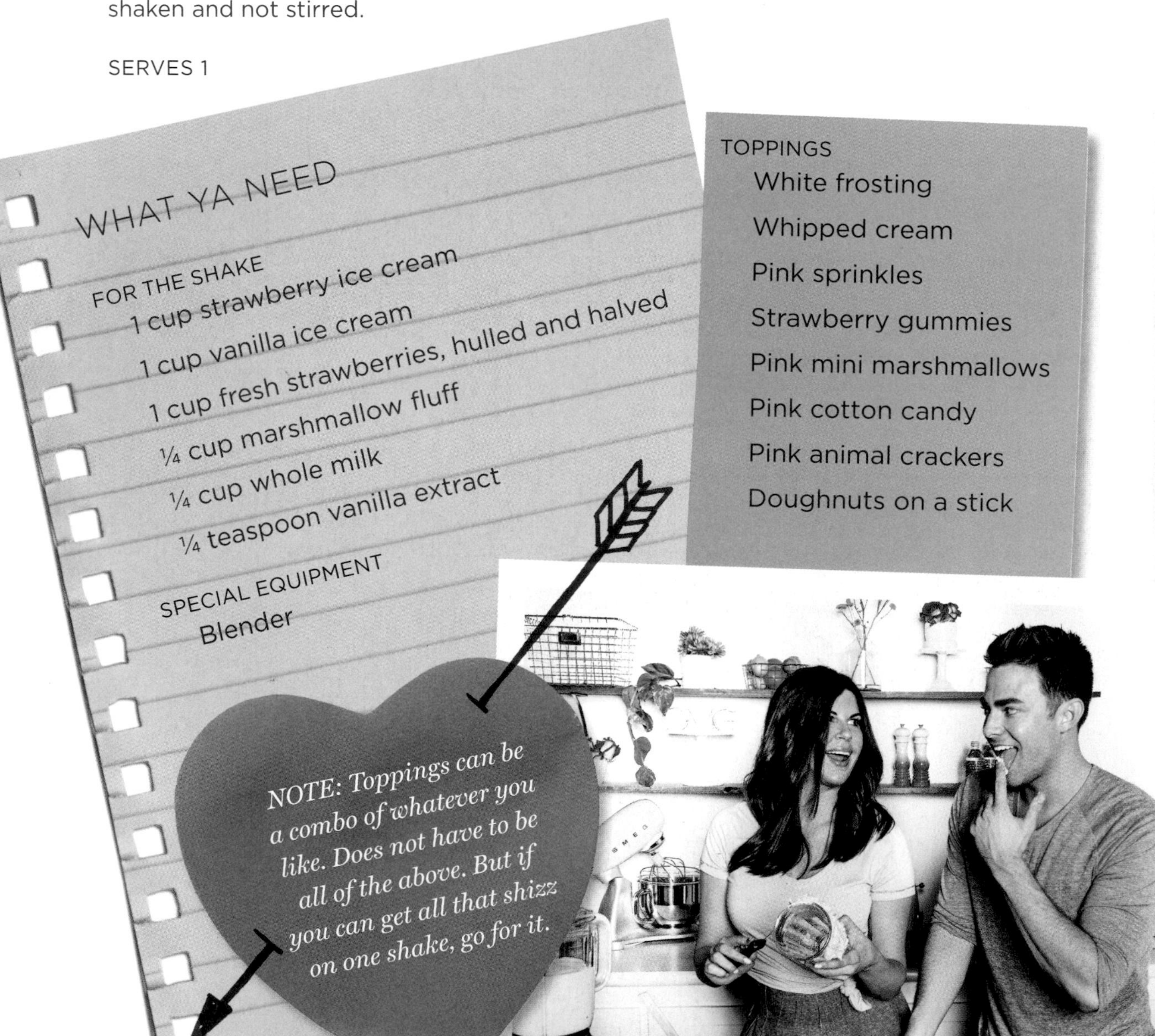

WHAT YA NEED

FOR THE SHAKE

- 1 cup strawberry ice cream
- 1 cup vanilla ice cream
- 1 cup fresh strawberries, hulled and halved
- ¼ cup marshmallow fluff
- ¼ cup whole milk
- ¼ teaspoon vanilla extract

SPECIAL EQUIPMENT

- Blender

TOPPINGS

- White frosting
- Whipped cream
- Pink sprinkles
- Strawberry gummies
- Pink mini marshmallows
- Pink cotton candy
- Pink animal crackers
- Doughnuts on a stick

NOTE: Toppings can be a combo of whatever you like. Does not have to be all of the above. But if you can get all that shizz on one shake, go for it.

- To start, you wanna prep your milkshake glass or vessel. Pick something tall and slender and get it chillin' in the freezer for 10 minutes before you start scooping. This will keep the shake cool and the frosting from melting.
- Spread a nice layer of thick frosting around the rim of your vessel, going down 2 to 3 inches. Now this is where the fun starts: Stack your favorite candies and treats all around that frosted rim—candy, doughnuts, cookies, sprinkles, anything goes.

- Now for the shake part. Combine all the shake ingredients in your blender and blend until smooth and creamy! Pour the shake into fully decorated glass, give it a hefty dose of whipped cream on top, and add in whatever else you got! Animal crackers? Fetch, yes! Cotton candy? Bring it! A lollipop the size of your face? Why not!! A slice of Cake Made of Rainbows and Smiles? DO IT . . . We dare you.

- And don't forget those IG-worthy adorable straws!

PS: You are soooo pretty with that whipped cream on your nose.

FINAL EXAM

Okay Plastics, it's time to see how much you really know about *Mean Girls*. So stop staring at Caroline Krafft's unplucked eyebrows and 99-cent lip gloss! It's time to focus!

Fill Me In

As the cool mom Mrs. George would say: What is the 411? What has everybody been up to? What is the hot gossip? Tell me everything. No seriously. Everything. You left out key words of these famous lines, and they need to be filled in, stat! See if you're cool enough to complete the deets.

Rules of Girl World

You can't wear a ________ two days in a row and you can only wear a ________ once a week. So I guess you picked today. Oh and we only wear jeans or ________ on Fridays. And if you break any of these rules, you can't sit with us at lunch.

Answer Key: tank top; ponytail; track pants

How Do I Even Begin to Describe Regina George

Regina George is ______. She has two ______ purses and a ______ Lexus. I hear her ______ is insured for $10,000. I hear she does car commercials in ______. Her favorite movie is ______. One time she met ______ on a plane. And he told her she was pretty. One time, she punched me in the face. It was awesome.

Answer Key: flawless; Fendi; silver; hair; Japan; Varsity Blues; John Stamos

Kevin Gnapoor's Rap

All you sucka emcees ain't got nothin' on me
From my ______, to my lines, you can't touch Kevin G.
I'm a Mathlete, the ______ is inferred
But forget what you heard, I'm like ______ the third
Sha-sha shaken, not ______, I'm Kevin Gnapoor
The G's ______ when I sneak in your door
I make love to your woman on the bathroom floor
I don't play it like ______, you'll know it was me
'Cause the next time you see her she'd be like
Ohhhhhh, Kevin G.!

Answer Key: grades; nerd; James Bond; stirred; silent; Shaggy

The Halloween Slut Rule

In the regular world, Halloween is when children dress up in ____________ and beg for candy. In ____________, Halloween is the one night a year where a girl can dress like a total ____________ and no other girls can say anything about it. The hardcore girls just wear ____________ and some form of ____________.

Answer Key: costumes; Girl World; slut; lingerie; animal ears

The Janis Burn

Let me tell you something about Janis Ian. We were best friends in ____________. I know, right? It's so embarrassing. I don't even—whatever. So then, in ____________ grade, I started going out with my first boyfriend ____________, who was totally gorgeous but then he moved to ____________. And Janis was, like, weirdly ____________ of him. If I would blow her off to hang out with Kyle, she would be like "why didn't you call me back?" and I'd be like "why are you so obsessed with me?" Then for my birthday party which was an all-girls (pool party) I was like "Janis, I can't invite you because I think you're a ____________."

Answer Key: middle school; eighth; Kyle; Indiana; jealous; lesbian

Ms. Norbury's Words of Wisdom

Cady, I know that having a ____________ may seem like the most important thing in the world right now, but you don't have to ____________ yourself down to get guys to like you. I know, how would I know, right? I'm ____________ ____________. I'm broke from getting ____________ from Chase Visa. And you know why? Because I'm a ____________. I push people. I pushed my husband into ____________. That was a bust. I pushed myself into working ____________ jobs. And now, I'm going to push you, because I know you're ____________ than that.

Answer Key: boyfriend; dumb; divorced; divorced; Randy; pusher; law school; three; smarter

Final Thoughts

WELL YOU MADE IT TO THE END OF THE BOOK and you didn't get hit by a bus. So, I would consider that a huge success. I hope you enjoyed reading this book as much as I enjoyed writing it. To say that being Aaron Samuels in *Mean Girls* changed my life is a big understatement. I have so much gratefulness in my heart for this film and for being able to be a part of it.

I admit at first, I didn't enjoy being called Aaron Samuels everywhere I went. People from all over, like baristas writing "Aaron" on my coffee cup, and teens running up and asking me if they could push my hair back, or if I could make them a video for their friend asking what day it was. (It's October 3rd.) The stigma was inescapable. Being Aaron Samuels even became annoying as an actor because I had done dozens of other films and TV shows and wanted to be known for much more than the guy who was victimized by Regina George. But as the love of *Mean Girls* grew and grew over the years so did my love of being Aaron Samuels. And I'll tell you when that really kicked in.

A few years before he died, I was at Applebee's with my father, David Bennett, who always liked to brag to waitresses about his son's acting accomplishments. After the meal, when he offered our waitress to take a photo of her and I, I'd had enough and got mad at him. Yes, I still smiled and took the photo with the young waitress, but when she giggled away I snapped at him, "Dad, can you not do that everywhere we go? I just want to eat dinner." I stormed out of the restaurant and sat in the car. A few moments later he walked out and said, "I know it can be annoying, Jon, but I want you to see something." He pointed inside through the window to where there were five girls hovering around a phone, giggling with huge smiles on their faces. One of them was even on the verge of tears.

"It might be annoying to you sometimes, but look at their faces, look how happy you just made them. When was the last time you saw someone that happy?" he said.

He was right.

The funny thing about *Mean Girls* that I've learned from fans over the years is that it's not just a movie, it's become a household name as well. It's a movie that is watched over and over countless times. Fans can quote almost every line of the movie, start to finish, and they use some of the quotes in life almost every day. It's the movie that you watch on repeat in your dorm when one of your girlfriends goes through a breakup. It's the only movie you want to watch when you're sick or hungover, lying on the couch covered in blankets. And the reason fans love it so much is because of the brilliant work of Tina Fey bringing characters and situations to life that everyone can relate to.

In addition, Tina brought awareness to bullying in high school in a creative comedic way, and that opened up the huge dialogue that started addressing the serious issue in high schools across the country. So, to all the fans who have been victimized by a Regina George: You are not alone. We see you, we hear you, and we will fight for you. The time for bullying is over.

I would like to thank you all, from the bottom of my heart, for letting me be a part of your life as Aaron Samuels. Thank you for pushing my hair back and thank you for lifting me up, and thank you for always supporting me.

Ya know I really didn't need to make a speech—gosh can I wrap it up?

Sure Mr. Duvall, I guess there's nothing left to say except: Grool.

Acknowledgments

I'd like to thank Marie (Reebs) Kovacs for showing me that the guac doesn't have to be regular it can be cool and for planting the pomegranate seed that became this book.

Thank you to my family. You know who you are.

I owe a huge thank-you to the most caring supportive team on the planet. Tiffany Kuzon, Kerri Ruddell, Craig Schneider, and Anthony Matteo. I don't know what I would do without you. You are the best.

Thank you to the team at Grand Central Publishing, and Brittany McInerney for believing in me and making this dream a reality.

Thank you to my niece Hannah Herner for helping her old uncle come up with games and quizzes that "the kids" would like and for writing them with me.

Thank you to Andrea Dana Eisen for helping write this book and for taking over when my attention span was no longer there (which was most of the time).

Thank you to Brent Weber Photo for always making me look good thanks to filter upon filter upon filter.

To my friends at Super Delicious and Food Network who got me into the cooking game, this couldn't happen without you. Cara Tapper, Adam Cohen, Joanna Vernetti, and Megan Lawrence you guys always allow me to shine and that takes trust, so thank you for your trust.

And finally to Jaymes, thank you for believing in me, loving me, and for always showing up. Thank you for THIS road and THIS adventure.

Additional Images

left (l), right (r), top (t), bottom (b), center (c)

i, 1 © Picsfive/Shutterstock.com

iii © Margaret M Stewart/ Shutterstock.com

v (t), vi (t r, t l), vii (t l), 15, 16, 18, 23, 33, 34, 39, 50 (t), 52, 66 (r), 70 (l), 76 (r), 89, 90 (r), 98 (t), 106 (r), 109 (r), 111, 114 (t), 124 (l), 131 (r), 132, 144 (r), 154, 156 (l), 160 (l) © happydancing/ Shutterstock.com

v (b), viii, 10, 14 (t r), 24, 64, 85, 92 (r), 96 (l), 112 (l), 124 (r), 131 (l), 138 (l), 141, 143, 148 (l), 161 (b), 162 (b) © natrot/ Shutterstock.com

vi (b l), vii (t r), ix, 12, 42, 50 (b), 55, 62 (t), 74, 92 (t l), 107, 120, 135, 144 (l), 152 (t) © DW labs Incorporated/Shutterstock.com

vi (b r), 40 (t l), 66 (l), 72 (l), 84, 87 (r), 90 (l), 94 (l), 99, 109 (l), 112 (r), 126, 130 (l), 138 (r), 146 (l), 160 (t r), 163 (t r) © RinUm/ Shutterstock.com

vii (b l), 14 (b l), 36 (r), 48 (r), 87 (l), 94 (r), 102, 123, 141 (b l), 161 (t), 162 (t) © Oleksii Khmyz/ Shutterstock.com

vii (b r), 14 (t l), 32, 68, 76 (l) © Stockforlife.com/Shutterstock.com

vii (wine stain) © Picsfive/Shutterstock.com

viii, 11, 37, 62 (b), 77 © SmartPhotoLab/Shutterstock.com

9, 31, 47, 61, 83, 105, 119, 137 © vanilla22/Shutterstock.com

14 (b r), 94 (b), 112 © Photo Melon/Shutterstock.com

25, 54 (b), 73, 104 © monbibi/ Shutterstock.com

26–27, 28–29, 44–45, 58–59, 80–81, 102–103 © Milanares/ Shutterstock.com

36 (l), 56 (r), 70 (r), 92 (b), 113, 122, 141 (r), 146 (r) © BK0808/ Shutterstock.com

38, 56 (l), 98 (b), 106 (l), 128, 22 © photastic/Shutterstock.com

40 (t r), 54 (t l), 72 (c), 96 (b r), 152 (b l) © Elnur/Shutterstock.com

43, 57, 95, 127 © Evgeny Karandaev/Shutterstock.com

45, 65, 100, 114 (b), 135 © grublee/Shutterstock.com

48 (l) and frame on 26, 58, 80, 102, 134 © Carolyn Franks/Shutterstock.com

51, 151 (t) © vesna cvorovic/ Shutterstock.com

66 (c), 72 (r) © ntstudio/Shutterstock.com

156 (heart), 20, 54 (t r), 64 (heart), 78, 96 (t r), 133, 141 (t), 148 (b), 151 (b) © Greenety/ Shutterstock.com

156 (r) © ConstantinosZ/Shutterstock.com

Index

A

Aaron Samuels, ix, x, 62, 77, 84, 89, 117, 164
Aaron Samuels, the, 117
Aaron Samuels's Actual Mom's Chicken Stuffed Shells, 84
Abercrombie & Fitch, 89
Africa Pepper Chicken, Hot as, 112
Africa Pepper Sauce, 112
alcoholic drinks (happy hour), 119
  Awesome Shooters, 126
  Half a Virgin Piña Colada, 132
  High Status Man-hattan Candy, 128
  Regulation Hottie Toddy, 122
  Strawberry Frosé, 74
  Test Results on the Rocks, 123
  Too Gay to Function Cosmo, 124
  Why Are You White? Russian, 120
  You Can't Sip with Us, 130
  You Go, Glenn (Hot) Coco, 131
All My Children, x
almond butter, in Swedish Nutrition Bars, 32
almond milk
  in You Smell Like a Baby Prosti-turmeric Latte, 55
  in You Will Get Pregnant and Diet Smoothie, 56
Amber D'Alessio Grilled Hot Dogs, 106
andouille sausage links, in JAMBO-laya, 87
angel hair pasta, 36
appetizers (whore d'oeuvres), 9
  Cheese and Crackers for Eight People, 20
  Gretchen's Wieners, 12
  I Can't Help That I'm So Popular Popcorn, 22
  It's Not Regular Guac, It's Cool Guac, 24
  So, You Agree? Fairy Toast, 10
  Spring Fling Rolls, 18
  Whatever, I'm Getting Cheese Fries, 14
  White Gold Hoops, 16
apples, in It's Not Regular Guac, It's Cool Guac, 24
appliances, 5
aprons, 2
Are Buttermilk Pancakes a Carb?, 34
avocados
  in It's Not Regular Guac, It's Cool Guac, 24
  in Whatever, I'm Getting Cheese Fries, 14
Awesome Shooters, 126

B

baby back ribs, in Best. Rack. Ever., 107
baguette, in Total Meltdown, 90
baking sheets, 4
Bars, Swedish Nutrition, 32
beans, in October 3-Bean White Chili, 94
beauty, DIY recipes, 44–45
beauty tips, 151
beef, ground
  in Everyone Grab Some RubBURGERs, 109
  in It's Like, All in Swedish Meatballs, 98
beets
  in deviled eggs, 64
  Give Me a Beet Hummus, 70
  Queen Beet-za, 72
  in Spring Fling Rolls, 18
Bennett, Ruthanne, xi, 84
berries, in Ms. Norberry Pie, 148
Best. Rack. Ever., 107
blenders, 5
Bloody Mary meatloaf, 96
Boo You Whore-iental Salad, 50
Boozy Burn Brunch, 134–35
Bowl, Homeschooled Jungle Veggie, 114
brain food, 83
  Aaron Samuels's Actual Mom's Chicken Stuffed Shells, 84
  It's Like, All in Swedish Meatballs, 98
  JAMBO-laya, 87
  October 3-Bean White Chili, 94
  She Asked Me How to Spell *Orange* Chicken, 92
  Total Meltdown, 90
  Why Are You So Obsessed with MEatloaf?, 96
burger, Everyone Grab Some RubBURGERs, 109
Burn Brunch Citrus Salad, 66
Buttermilk Pancakes a Carb?, Are, 34

C

cabbbage
  in Boo You Whore-iental Salad, 50
  in Not Word Salad. Actual Pink Salad, 76
  in Spring Fling Rolls, 18
Caboodle, 2
Cady, the, 116
Cady Heron, 31, 53, 54, 77, 80, 113, 116
  Plastics Pop Quiz, 26–29
Caesar Salad, Just Stab, 48
Cake Made of Rainbows and Smiles, 138
cakes
  Cake Made of Rainbows and Smiles, 138
  Fun-Fetchy Cake, 141
cast iron pans, 4
Chabert, Lacey, viii, 144
Cheese and Crackers for Eight People, 20
Cheese Fries, Whatever, I'm Getting, 14
cheesy toasts, Total Meltdown, 90
Cherrios, in Do Not Trust These Treats, 78
chicken
  Aaron Samuels's Actual Mom's Chicken Stuffed Shells, 84
  Hot as Africa Pepper Chicken, 112
  in JAMBO-laya, 87
  She Asked Me How to Spell *Orange* Chicken, 92
Chili, October 3-Bean White, 94
Christensen, Kaylen, 111
Citrus Champagne Vinaigrette, 76

Citrus Salad, Burn Brunch, 66
Coconut Face Cream, 44
coconut milk
in Half a Virgin Piña Colada, 132
in You Smell Like a Baby Prosti-turmeric Latte, 55
coleslaw mix, in I'm Sorry People Are So Jealous of My Perfect Pink Taco, 68
cooking oils, 6–7
corn, in Whatever, I'm Getting Cheese Fries, 14
cornbread, Is Your Cornbread Muffin Buttered?, 42
Cosmo, Too Gay to Function, 124
Crack Rock Candy, 154
cramming for finals. *See* brain food
Cranberry Fat Flush, Three-Days-'til-Spring Fling, 54

D

Damian and Janis, the, 117
Damian Leigh, 29, 51, 61, 117, 124
desserts, 137
Cake Made of Rainbows and Smiles, 138
Crack Rock Candy, 154
Do Not Trust These Treats, 78
Face Smells Like a Foot Peppermint Bark, 144
Fun-Fetchy Cake, 141
Hump Day Treat: Peanut Butter BALLS, 146
Milkshake-It Like 2004, 156
Ms. Norberry Pie, 148
Strawberry Toaster Doodles, 152
deviled, eggs, She's Fabulous, but She's Evil. And These Are Her Deviled Eggs, 64
diets. *See* Regina's All-Carb Diet; weight loss recipes
DIY beauty, 44–45
Do Not Trust These Treats, 78
Drinking Game, Four to Six, 134
drinks
Awesome Shooters, 126
Half a Virgin Piña Colada, 132
High Status Man-hattan Candy, 128
Milkshake-It Like 2004, 156
Regulation Hottie Toddy, 122
Strawberry Frosé, 74
Test Results on the Rocks, 123
Three-Days-'til-Spring Fling Cranberry Fat Flush, 54
Too Gay to Function Cosmo, 124
Why Are You White? Russian, 120
You Can't Sip with Us, 130
You Go, Glenn (Hot) Coco, 131
You Smell Like a Baby Prosti-turmeric Latte, 55
You Will Get Pregnant and Diet Smoothie, 56

E

Everyone Grab Some RubBURGERs, 109
extra virgin olive oil, 6

F

Face Cream, Coconut, 44
Face Smells Like a Foot Peppermint Bark, 144
Fairy Toast, So, You Agree?, 10
farro, in Homeschooled Jungle Veggie Bowl, 114
"fat ass," 15
"fetch," ix, 31
Fetch-uccini Alfredo, 38
Fill in the Blanks Final Exam, 160–63
final exam, 160–63
finals. *See* brain food
flour, 7
food processors, 5
Four to Six Drinking Game, 134
Frosé, Strawberry, 74
Full-of-Secrets Hair Volumizing Mask, 45
Fun-Fetchy Cake, 141
Funfetti Cake Mix, in Fun-Fetchy Cake, 141

G

games
Fill in the Blanks Final Exam, 160–63
Mean Girls MASH, 80–81
Gazpacho, I Want My Pink Soup Back! Watermelon, 62
Give Me a Beet Hummus, 70
Glenn Coco, 9, 131, 152
Gretchen, the, 116
Gretchen's Wieners, 12
Gretchen Wieners, viii, 12, 38, 58, 116, 131, 152
Plastics Pop Quiz, 26–29
grilled meats, 105
Amber D'Alessio Grilled Hot Dogs, 106
Best. Rack. Ever., 107
Everyone Grab Some RubBURGERs, 109
Hot as Africa Pepper Chicken, 112
Grool Sleepover Oats, 52
Gruyère cheese, in Total Meltdown, 90
guacamole, It's Not Regular Guac, It's Cool Guac, 24

H

Hair Volumizing Mask, Full-of-Secrets, 45
Half a Virgin Piña Colada, 132
Halloween Slut Rule, 162
hand mixers, 5
happy hour, 119
Awesome Shooters, 126
Half a Virgin Piña Colada, 132
High Status Man-hattan Candy, 128
Regulation Hottie Toddy, 122
Strawberry Frosé, 74
Test Results on the Rocks, 123
Too Gay to Function Cosmo, 124
Why Are You White? Russian, 120
You Can't Sip with Us, 130
You Go, Glenn (Hot) Coco, 131
High Status Man-hattan Candy, 128
Hill, Dwayne, 57
Homeschooled Jungle Veggie Bowl, 114
hors d'oeuvres. *See* whore d'oeuvres
Hot as Africa Pepper Chicken, 112
(Hot) Coco, You Go, Glenn, 131
hot dogs
Amber D'Alessio Grilled Hot Dogs, 106
Lit'l Smokies sausages, in Gretchen's Wieners, 12
Hottie Toddy, Regulation, 122
Hummus, Give Me a Beet, 70
Hump Day Treat: Peanut Butter BALLS, 146

I

I Can't Help That I'm So Popular Popcorn, 22
ice cream, in Milkshake-It Like 2004, 156
I'm Sorry People Are So Jealous of My Perfect Pink Taco, 68
Is Your Cornbread Muffin Buttered?, 42
It's Like, All in Swedish Meatballs, 98
It's Not Regular Guac, It's Cool Guac, 24
I Want My Pink Soup Back! Watermelon Gazpacho, 62

J

JAMBO-laya, 87
Janis Burn, the, 162
Janis Ian, 29, 90, 117, 137, 162
Jason, the, 117
"Jingle Bell Rock," 59, 103, 134
Just Stab Caesar Salad, 48

K

Karen, the, 117
Karen Smith, 10, 21, 31, 52, 80, 117
  Plastics Pop Quiz, 26–29
Kevin G., 70, 117, 127, 161
Kevin Gnapoor, the, 117
Kevin Gnapoor's Rap, 70, 161
kitchen essentials, 2–5
knives, 4

L

Lit'l Smokies sausages, in Gretchen's Wieners, 12
Lohan, Lindsay, ix, 51, 54, 62, 111

M

Mac and Cheese Balls, Because I'm a Mouse, Duh, 40
mandarin oranges
  in Boo You Whore-iental Salad, 50
  in Burn Brunch Citrus Salad, 66
Man-hattan Candy, High Status, 128
marshmallows
  in Do Not Trust These Treats, 78
  I Can't Help That I'm So Popular Popcorn, 22
Martin, Nikki, xi
McAdams, Rachel, ix, 15, 23, 54, 65, 106
Meadows, Tim, 146
Mean Girls, viii, ix, x, xi, 11, 114, 164–65
Mean Girls MASH, 80–81
Mean Girls Workout, 58–59
measuring cups and spoons, 4
Meatballs, It's Like, All in Swedish, 98
MEatloaf?, Why Are You So Obsessed with, 96
Milkshake-It Like 2004, 156
Moscato, in Awesome Shooters, 126
Ms. Norberry Pie, 148
Ms. Norbury's Words of Wisdom, 163

N

nonstick pans, 4
North Shore High School Class Superlatives, 116–17
Not Word Salad. Actual Pink Salad, 76

O

oats
  Grool Sleepover Oats, 52
  in Swedish Nutrition Bars, 32
Obama, Barack, 39
October 3-Bean White Chili, 94
onion rings, White Gold Hoops, 16
Orange Chicken, She Asked Me How to Spell, 92

P

pancakes, Are Buttermilk Pancakes a Carb?, 34
pancetta, in Total Meltdown, 90
pans, 4
pantry essentials, 6–7
pasta
  Aaron Samuels's Actual Mom's Chicken Stuffed Shells, 84
  Fetch-uccini Alfredo, 38
  Mac and Cheese Balls, Because I'm a Mouse, Duh, 40
  Your (Angel) Hair Looks Sexy Pushed Back, 36
peanut butter, in Swedish Nutrition Bars, 32
Peanut Butter BALLS, 146
peanuts, in Boo You Whore-iental Salad, 50
Peppermint Bark, Face Smells Like a Foot, 144
Pie, Ms. Norberry, 148
pink, 61
pink recipes
  Burn Brunch Citrus Salad, 66
  Do Not Trust These Treats, 78
  Give Me a Beet Hummus, 70
  I Can't Help That I'm So Popular Popcorn, 22
  I'm Sorry People Are So Jealous of My Perfect Pink Taco, 68
  I Want My Pink Soup Back! Watermelon Gazpacho, 62
  Not Word Salad. Actual Pink Salad, 76
  Queen Beet-za, 72
  She's Fabulous, but She's Evil. And These Are Her Deviled Eggs, 64
  Strawberry Frosé, 74
pizza, Queen Beet-za, 72
Pizza-Face Skin Clearing Mask, 45
Planned Parenthood, 64, 123
Plastics Pop Quiz, 26–29
PMA (positive mental attitude), 2
Poehler, Amy, 25, 146
Popcorn, I Can't Help That I'm So Popular, 22
Pop Quizzes
  Duh (True) or Shut Up (False)?, 102–3
  Which Plastic Are You?, 26–29
pork
  baby back ribs, in Best. Rack. Ever., 107
  ground, in It's Like, All in Swedish Meatballs, 98

Q

Queen Bees and Wannabes (Wiseman), 73
Queen Beet-za, 72

R

radicchio, in Not Word Salad. Actual Pink Salad, 76
radishes, in Not Word Salad. Actual Pink Salad, 76
Regina, the, 117

Regina George, 15, 16, 17, 31, 54, 62, 161
  Plastics Pop Quiz, 26–29
Regina's All-Carb Diet, 31
  Are Buttermilk Pancakes a Carb?, 34
  Fetch-uccini Alfredo, 38
  Is Your Cornbread Muffin Buttered?, 42
  Mac and Cheese Balls, Because I'm a Mouse, Duh, 40
  Swedish Nutrition Bars, 32
  Your (Angel) Hair Looks Sexy Pushed Back, 36
Regulation Hottie Toddy, 122
rice cookers, 5
rice paper wrappers, in Spring Fling Rolls, 18
rosé
  Strawberry Frosé, 74
  in You Can't Sip with Us, 130
rules for being a Plastic, 61

S

safety tip, 7
salads
  Boo You Whore-iental Salad, 50
  Burn Brunch Citrus Salad, 66
  Just Stab Caesar Salad, 48
  Not Word Salad. Actual Pink Salad, 76
salt, 2, 4
She Asked Me How to Spell *Orange* Chicken, 92
She's Fabulous, but She's Evil. And These Are Her Deviled Eggs, 64
shrimp, in I'm Sorry People Are So Jealous of My Perfect Pink Taco, 68
Skanky Saturday Skin Detox Mask, 44
Skin-Brightening Face Mask, Spring Fling's This Weekend!, 45
Skin Clearing Mask, Pizza-Face, 45
Skin Detox Mask, Skanky Saturday, 44
Smoothie, You Will Get Pregnant and Diet, 56
spices, 7
spinach
  in Homeschooled Jungle Veggie Bowl, 114
  in You Will Get Pregnant and Diet Smoothie, 56
Spring Fling Rolls, 18
Spring Fling's This Weekend! Skin-Brightening Face Mask, 45
Strawberry Frosé, 74
Strawberry Toaster Doodles, 152
Swedish lesson, 100
Swedish Meatballs, It's Like, All in, 98
Swedish Nutrition Bars, 32
sweet corn, in Whatever, I'm Getting Cheese Fries, 14
sweet potato fries, in Whatever, I'm Getting Cheese Fries, 14

T

Taco, I'm Sorry People Are So Jealous of My Perfect Pink, 68
Test Results on the Rocks, 123
Three-Days-'til-Spring Fling Cranberry Fat Flush, 54
Toaster Doodles, Strawberry, 152
toasts
  cheesy toasts, Total Meltdown, 90
  So, You Agree? Fairy Toast, 10
tofu, in Spring Fling Rolls, 18
Too Gay to Function Cosmo, 124
Total Meltdown, 90
True of False quiz, 102–3
turkey, ground, in Why Are You So Obsessed with MEatloaf?, 96

V

Veggie Bowl, Homeschooled Jungle, 114
Virgin Piña Colada, Half a, 132
vomit scene, 77

W

Watermelon Gazpacho, I Want My Pink Soup Back!, 62
weight loss, 47
weight loss recipes
  Boo You Whore-iental Salad, 50
  Grool Sleepover Oats, 52
  Just Stab Caesar Salad, 48
  Three-Days-'til-Spring Fling Cranberry Fat Flush, 54
  You Smell Like a Baby Prosti-turmeric Latte, 55
You Will Get Pregnant and Diet Smoothie, 56
Whatever, I'm Getting Cheese Fries, 14
White Chili, October 3-Bean, 94
White Gold Hoops, 16
White? Russian, Why Are You, 120
whore d'oeuvres, 9
  Cheese and Crackers for Eight People, 20
  Gretchen's Wieners, 12
  I Can't Help That I'm So Popular Popcorn, 22
  It's Not Regular Guac, It's Cool Guac, 24
  So, You Agree? Fairy Toast, 10
  Spring Fling Rolls, 18
  Whatever, I'm Getting Cheese Fries, 14
  White Gold Hoops, 16
Why Are You So Obsessed with MEatloaf?, 96
Why Are You White? Russian, 120
"wide-set vagina," 43
witch hazel, about, 45
Workout, *Mean Girls*, 58–59

Y

yelllow squash, in Homeschooled Jungle Veggie Bowl, 114
You Can't Sip with Us, 130
You Go, Glenn (Hot) Coco, 131
Your (Angel) Hair Looks Sexy Pushed Back, 36
You Smell Like a Baby Prosti-turmeric Latte, 55
You Will Get Pregnant and Diet Smoothie, 56

Z

zucchini, in Homeschooled Jungle Veggie Bowl, 114

About the Authors

Jonathan Bennett

He's not just another guy who looks sexy with his hair pushed back. No, Jonathan Bennett is a multi-talented actor who always wants to know what day it is (October 3rd). Oh, and he's also bad at math. Originally from Toledo, Ohio (no, he wasn't homeschooled), Bennett currently resides full-time in Los Angeles, where he has worked steadily as an actor and host for over fifteen years.

After being cast by Lorne Michaels and Tina Fey in the blockbuster hit movie *Mean Girls,* he went on to play opposite Amanda Bynes in *Lovewrecked* and as the antagonistic son-in-law of Steve Martin in *Cheaper by the Dozen 2.* He also starred as Bo Duke in the Warner Bros. prequel to *The Dukes of Hazzard,* in the comedy romp *Bachelor Party Vegas,* and as the title role of National Lampoon's *Van Wilder: Freshman Year.* He

also loves to take on private projects with grittier themes that take him out of his comfort zone.

Strutting his moves on the dance floor, Jonathan also became a fan favorite on *Dancing with the Stars* in 2015, which was the inspiration for a whole new set of memes on social media featuring his facial expressions. We know, we know, that's pretty grool. Jonathan is now a staple on the Food Network as host of one of its top rated shows, *Cake Wars.* Although he isn't a baker, he does love his cake, and eating it too (not just the ones baked out of rainbows and smiles).

Nikki Martin

Nikki Martin was born and raised in Southern California and has had a modern love affair with all things edible and drinkable since a very young age. Nikki has also always loved the bright lights and being on stage. When she was eighteen, she moved to Hollywood to pursue a career in acting. She says her *Mean Girls* spirit animal is a combo of Gretchen and Cady and that there should be a spin-off movie about Glenn Coco, or maybe Seth Mosakowski.

Nikki's sassy skills can be seen on the big screen in Touchstone's hit comedy *Sorority Boys,* where she played an oh-so-popular, yet skanky Tri Pi, but wished her army of skanks were as loyal as Regina's. Although the flick was a hit, her career took a turn when she realized she loved food and cooking more than fishing for Hump Day Treats at craft services. Nikki was soon "discovered" as a rad chick who could throw an insanely amazing dinner party and was swooped up by some A-list celebs to be their personal chef. After taking some time to run the ovens and grills of the rich and famous, Nikki headed back to the Hollywood lights as a chef on several lifestyle shows for Food Network, Bravo, HGTV, and more. She even founded one of the coolest, and most exclusive, invite-only dinner clubs: The Roulette Society.

Today, Nikki is most notably known as the "Grill Next Door" from *Food Network Star* season 8, where she was the finalist that gave Bobby Flay a run for his money on grilling. She is also a huge *Mean Girls* fan and when her parents told her they were going out of town and staying overnight while attending a Ladysmith Black Mambazo concert, she jumped at the opportunity to create the collection of recipes for *The Burn Cookbook.*

HEY

Inspired to rally your Plastics, cook something grool, and eat your feelings? Why not let it out and put it in the book, honey? Snap a 'Gram and show us the goods!

#BurnCookBook Besties

#PlasticsLoveFrosé

On Wednesdays We Eat, Drink, and Wear Pink

Does She Even Grill Here?

#MeanGrills

I ♡ Aaron Samuels

#BurnBrunch